WHAT OTHERS ARE SAYING...

"The Winning Mindset *is a winner! The principles in this book have been gleaned from years of experiences and conversations. David Welday is the ideal person to speak on having a winning attitude because he lives it. This is one book you'll refer to time and again."*
Hal Donaldson, President, Convoy of Hope

"This book invites leaders to do more than lead—it dares leaders to apply healthy principles with the right attitude, seeing everything from the best view. Isn't that what we want to do? Isn't that what works best? I believe so. Open the book. Open your mind. And lead correctly."
Chris Maxwell, Author, Pastor, Speaker

"Life can soil the soul. The Winning Mindset *is like a box of heart wipes for cleansing the spirit. Each vignette carries the possibility for righting a wrong attitude of the heart while bringing out our best qualities."*
Kevin W. McCarthy, Author, *The On-Purpose Person* **and** *Making Your Life Make Sense*

"David Welday offers consistently sound as well as uplifting insights into how to gain altitude through your attitude. I highly recommend his work as both an author and long-time associate."
Laurie Beth Jones, Author of *Jesus CEO* **and** *Jesus Life Coach*

"*The Winning Mindset is an amazing compilation of wisdom that will help you meet and exceed your next big goal or mission. David shares tips that will help you avoid things such as falling into the comparison trap, letting fear drive you, or getting sidetracked or distracted from your set mission. Each lesson will keep you marching in the right direction toward your set goals.*"
Mo Mydlo, Speaker, Author, and President, Unforsaken Ministries

"*This is a brilliant compilation of inspirational and motivational thoughts that the author has gleaned through his years of experience as a sought-after speaker, as well as a professional writer. The book is an easy read that gives the reader meaningful insights in the development of right attitudes and perspectives to life's daily encounters.*"
Elizabeth (Beth) Grant, PhD,
Executive Presbyter, Assemblies of God
Executive Director, Project Rescue

"*A leader in the art of professional development and personal transformation, author, publisher, and change-management expert, David Welday has produced an exceptional book that will inspire and motivate the masses.* The Winning Mindset *will enhance the effectiveness of the most seasoned leader, as well as those new to leadership and relationships. Welday has taken some difficult leadership concepts and simplified them into a leadership-development regimen. Concepts such as 'knowing your blind spots' and 'push through your fears' are a must-read for all leaders!*"
Dr. Clarence Nixon, Founder,
T-Labs Accelerated Learning Systems

THE
WINNING MINDSET

THE
WINNING
MINDSET

How to approach people, problems, and
situations and come out on top!

DAVID WELDAY

Published by HigherLife Development Services, Inc.
PO Box 623307
Oviedo, Florida 32762
www.ahigherlife.com

Copyright © 2022 David W. Welday III
ISBN: 978-1-954533-13-4 (Paperback)
978-1-954533-14-1 (ebook)
Library of Congress Control Number: 2021904786

Printed in the United States of America.
10 9 8 7 6 5 4 3 2 1

TABLE OF
CONTENTS

INTRODUCTION

"You can't always control circumstances. However, you can always control your attitude, approach, and response."

— TONY DUNGY

Why are some people seemingly more blessed or successful than others? Why do some seem to catch all the breaks? If you've managed to survive past adolescence, congratulations! You now realize that life just isn't fair. We are not all dealt an equal hand. Yet despite the outward circumstances that life brings, regardless of whether you were born with a silver spoon or a wooden spoon in your mouth, the fact is, some people simply do better in life than others. Often, those who grew up with the most challenging of circumstances manage to live much of their adult lives with significance, purpose, and joy. This is true in our personal lives as well as in our business lives. I believe that in the heart of every man and woman is a desire, a longing, to live well. This book will help you on that journey. I don't pretend to offer any foolproof solutions to experiencing a wonderful life. What I can share with you are some simple, learnable, embraceable principles that will help you live better. This book contains sixty-seven strategies for adopting the "Winning Mindset" in your life—a positive attitude that will improve your life in immeasurable ways. I recommend using this book as a devotional or personal improvement plan where you focus on one strategy at a time. These strategies all relate to attitude—how you think about the circumstances you face. Whether you are conquering the fears that hold you back, communicating with your family or clients, or struggling to adapt to change, attitude, or mindset, is the common denominator that will transcend all other factors to propel you forward. You've probably heard the phrase, "Attitude is everything." That may not be precisely true, but it's close. How you approach any circumstance in terms of your mindset, beliefs, and choices has a tremendous impact on the ultimate outcome. Even when your circumstances don't improve, your emotional courage, confidence, stability, and strength can. Do I have it all figured out? Not at all. Like you, I am on my own path, my own journey. In many respects, you might be far ahead of me on the life-satisfaction scale. You might have more money, more popularity, more influence. Good for you. Still, I believe the simple principles and stories I share with you in the ensuing pages will help you live better. Maybe just one chapter, one simple idea, will make all the difference you need to take your level of joy and peace to a new, higher level. When that happens, I will be satisfied. It is my earnest desire that the insights in this book will help you experience the thrill of living a difference ... a difference that will satisfy your soul and improve your life. Sometimes that difference is indefinable. Sometimes it's indescribable. Nevertheless, the right attitude can and will make a difference that will benefit you and those around you! Here's to your highest and best...

— DAVID WELDAY

Look Up— See Where You're Heading

W e've all seen it. Most of us have done it—found ourselves walking or perhaps in the midst of a conversation with our head down, focused on our phone, reading or responding to a text.

It's an all-too-common habit for many of us. This picture is symbolic of what I think is a greater challenge. In today's fast-paced, media-saturated culture, we can easily get into this myopic mindset where we are primarily focused on what's immediately in front of us. Our heads are down and we are piling through our to-do list and daily tasks without regard for the longer-range focus on where we are heading.

Recently I was on a leadership panel and I found myself asking the question, "What makes a person a leader?" I'm sure there are many facets to that answer, but one of the "biggies" is *the ability to see where you need to be heading, cast the vision for that, and inspire others to follow you in getting there.* Leaders "see." They have vision for what's possible. Their heads are up. Their eyes are on the prize, focusing forward. They not only have passion to get from where they are to where they need to be. They have the drive and discipline it takes to get there. They also understand that getting there alone is not acceptable. They want and need others to join them on this quest.

So my questions for you today are: Where are you called to lead? How clearly do you "see" where you need to get to, compared to where you are? How are you doing in casting the vision for what you see for others? What action steps are you taking to inspire and bring others along?

Maybe we all need to lift up our heads just a bit more often and look forward instead of down.

YOU Are a Source of Incredible Wealth

I figured this title would grab your attention. Why? Because most of us don't think of ourselves as wealthy. Oh sure, we are comfortable. We have more than most, and we should be thankful for our blessings, for what we do have.

But as you are thankful for your many blessings, I want to encourage you to focus on the "giving" portion of the word thanksgiving. Yes, it is important to be thankful for your blessings, for what you have. But you are made to be a contributor, a provider, a conduit of blessing to others. You are made to be a giver. You have incredible gifts, talents, abilities, and experience—a unique combination of these things unlike any other person in the world. There are things to be done that only you can do. There are problems to be solved that only you can solve. There are people to be helped and lifted up who only you can reach.

So this week, by all means take time to pause, to reflect, to consider all the things for which you are thankful. But don't stop there. Ask yourself, "What can I do this week to make the most impact in the world?" Maybe it's making sure your kids know they are loved and valued. You can do that like no other. Maybe there is a well in Africa that won't be dug without your support. Maybe there is a co-worker who is hurting right now and needs a friend or an opportunity or training that only you can provide.

My friend, YOU are a source of incredible wealth. You are blessed not just to be thankful but to be purposefully used to be a blessing to others.

Things grow when they are planted. Money grows when it's invested. Your personal riches of time, talent, and treasure, education, and experience will increase as you give them away.

Use who you are and what you have to make a difference in the world today.

The Path You Don't Want to Take

Y ou and I are on a path, a journey. We are headed somewhere. Perhaps you are an intentional person; you think about where you want to go and you pursue that path diligently. Oh sure, you get hit with setbacks and detours along the way. Who doesn't? But you try to be relentless in pursuing your chosen path.

Maybe your life is not quite so planned. You tend to default to taking life as it comes. You resist setting goals and prefer to stay "in the moment" and let life come to you. You value spontaneity and flexibility over schedules and goals.

Regardless of how you approach life, relationships, and business, you are still journeying through it. You are on a path.

So what's the path you might want to avoid?

It's the path of least resistance. Now sometimes the easy way, the obvious way, indeed is the best way forward.

But that's usually not the case. Like it or not, the way we get ahead in life, the way we deal with life, is through resistance.

Planes prefer to take off and land heading into the wind, not with the wind behind them. Why? The resistance of the air flowing faster over the top of the wing than the air flowing under the wing is what creates the lift that causes the plane to fly at all. If you spend any time in the gym, you understand that to gain strength, to build muscle, you have to endure resistance. You have to lift a weight or stretch a band that is pulling against you. We exist in an atmosphere that provides a constant resistance known as gravity that holds us down. All movement forward, whether on a bicycle or a car, is moving against the resistance of that gravitational pull.

One of the downfalls of many organizations, be it a corporation, a church, a school, or a non-profit charity, is when the gifted and strong leader who helped build and lead the organization becomes surrounded by people who only agree with the leader. They become "yes men" (or women), who whether out of fear, or a desire to kiss up, always agree with the boss. They are great at providing affirmation. A needed trait. But there's no resistance—no one to question the status quo or the leader's direction. Great leaders know that they need to be challenged, questioned. They rely on critical thinking, the outside and sometimes contrary perspectives, to land at the best decision. When leaders become surrounded with people who only "kiss up," who only agree with them, something is lost. Blind spots become acceptable. Innovation takes a back seat to preserving the status quo because the status quo is good; it's comfortable.

Take some time to ask yourself, "Do I have people in my life, on my team, who will provide resistance when it's needed? Am I creating a culture, an atmosphere that celebrates, even rewards speaking up, thinking differently, and challenging the status quo?" If you don't like the answer, make the decision today to change some things. Add some resistance to your life. That's a path that can lead to greatness!

Five "Mistakes" That Became Brilliant Ideas

You've undoubtedly heard the phrase, "One man's trash is another man's treasure." The fact is that sometimes our best ideas are born from the substance of our biggest blunders.

Well, here are some noteworthy ideas that started out as something, well, let's just say, less impressive.

1. Cornflakes—The Kellogg Brothers, John and Will, were just trying to boil a pot of grain. They inadvertently left the pot on the stove too long and the grain dried up and became hard and moldy. Well, the brothers worked on eliminating the mold and wound up creating one of the most popular brands of breakfast cereal of all time.

2. The Microwave Oven—Percy Spencer was an engineer at Raytheon Corporation. He was doing research related to radars using a new vacuum tube. Spencer noticed that the candy bar in his pocket began to melt during one of his experiments.

He then put popcorn into the machine. When it started to pop, he knew he had stumbled onto something significant.

3. Kermit the Frog—In 1955 Betty Henson had an old green coat she no longer wanted, and threw it out. Her son Jim took the coat and made it into a puppet, slicing a ping-pong ball in half to make the eyes. Thus was the beginning of Kermit the Frog, the beloved Sesame Street character.

4. Post-it Notes—A researcher at 3M, Spencer Silver, was working to create a strong adhesive. In the process, he noticed one of his efforts didn't have very much "sticking power" but didn't leave any marks or residue either. Years later a colleague spread the substance on little pieces of paper to mark his place in his choir hymn book, and the idea was born.

5. Penicillin—Scottish physician Alexander Fleming was seeking to create a drug that would cure diseases. He wasn't having much luck. However, Fleming noticed that a contaminated Petri dish he discarded contained a mold that was dissolving all the bacteria around it. He grew the mold by itself, and penicillin was discovered.

Maybe you don't have the world's next brilliant novel or notable scientific discovery sitting in your desk drawer or your waste can—but then, maybe you do? The moral of the story here is to keep your eyes open. Look for undiscovered opportunity and blessing that may be sitting right under your nose. Don't give up. Maybe the solution or breakthrough you've been looking for is just around the corner!

Are You Teachable?

Recently I spoke to a group of up-and-coming leaders on the subject of being "teachable." You'd think at my age, being teachable is not as critical a skill or character trait. But the truth is, at every age and season of life, we should be open to learn, willing to be wrong, and interested in expanding our horizons and skill set.

The good news is that being teachable is not something you are born with. It's a learned skill. That means you have no excuse to not be teachable. Being teachable is unlike athleticism or the ability to process information quickly, traits that while valuable, are not distributed evenly to every person. You can learn to be more teachable. What does it take to be teachable? Here are my observations on four things that will help you be a teachable person.

> **1. Humility—**If you are more concerned about what others think, about your reputation, than learning something new, than being better, you won't be very teachable.

2. Confidence—Again, be willing to admit you don't know everything. Put yourself out there and be vulnerable by asking questions. This takes a certain level of self-confidence. You have to be more interested in growing and getting better than preserving whatever level of positive perception you believe others have of you.

3. Vision—Teachable people tend to live with a sense of vision and mission. They recognize that their life matters. They are pursuing a dream. In pursuit of that dream, that mission, that sense of life purpose, they are willing to ask questions. They are willing to be teachable and risk their reputation in the hopes of getting better and getting closer to their goals. There is a proverb found in the Bible that says, "Fools take no pleasure in understanding but delight in airing their own opinions" (Prov. 18:2). Ouch!

4. Listen—Nobody gets better by talking. Ask questions. Listen. You will be surprised what you can learn. In listening to and honoring the opinions of others, you will likely find that your own relational stock rises. People appreciate and respect a person who is willing to listen to them. You may find that forcing yourself to listen first and ask questions allows you to let go of outdated ideas and information and more quickly embrace new thinking that can help you get better and get where you want to go.

So this week, take a few moments to do some personal inventory. On a scale of one to ten how teachable are you? Are there areas where you have perhaps resisted change or dug in your heels saying, "It's my way or the highway"? How might being more teachable add to your character and skill set?

How Well Are You Managing Your Margin?

As a publisher, I'm used to reviewing books from a variety of perspectives. One perspective is how does the book look? Not just the front cover mind you, but how inviting is the interior design? One thing that is a turn-off to me is if the book has very narrow margins. Think about it, if you picked up a book and the words filled the entire page from top to bottom, right to left, chances are, you would not want to read that book. It's simply too crowded. There is no margin.

In many ways, our lives are like the pages of a book. We can fill up our days, our weeks, our months with so much activity, so much busyness that we no longer have any margin. When that happens, we get stressed out, even sick. We lose our joy. We make more mistakes. Perhaps the biggest loss is that we miss out on new opportunities. Last minute tickets to a ballgame. A longtime friend pops into town unexpectedly. A chance to meet with an influential prospective client is passed up. A friend who is hurting and needs some time with you gets put off.

We need margin in our life. We need time to recharge, space to re-energize, room to breathe.

Yes, I know that taking time for a walk, to pause and pray, to watch a movie, to take a nap, to just wander the house and think seems horribly inefficient. But to fail to create margin in your life is even more inefficient. We need margin. A painting or a promotion that is filled with too much clutter, too many words, too much design, too much "stuff" is not attractive. Designers know that the artful use of "white space" is important. Musicians know that a good music composition needs rests—those blank spaces on the sheet music where no notes are played or sung.

So my challenge to you today is simply this: Take a few minutes to look at your schedule for this week. Other than the time when you are sawing logs, where is your margin? Where are your spaces and places of rest and recharging? Where are the planned holes in your calendar that can either stay vacant or be used to take advantage of an unexpected opportunity that may come up?

Lead with Gratitude

I like taking personality tests—Myers Briggs, StrengthsFinder, Enneagram, DISC — I'm sure there are others. Probably the one I've used the most is the DISC test which gives you a "score" in these four areas:

1. **Dominant**—change-agents, leaders, extroverted, task-oriented

2. **Inspiring**—outgoing, communicators, extroverted, people-oriented

3. **Supportive**—reliable, consistent, stable, introverted, people-oriented

4. **Cautious**—analytical, critical thinkers, introverted, task-oriented

Whenever I take this test, I score way high on the first two, the "D" and the "I". Now every personality type has strengths and weaknesses. The key is to recognize them and focus on enhancing your strengths and minimizing your weaknesses.

One area I am currently working on is to be more intentional to express my appreciation, my gratitude to the people who contribute to my life, the people with whom I work, play, worship, and interact. I find that in my zeal to get things done, to make a difference, its easy to focus so much on the tasks at hand that I sometimes fail to take the time to stop and say, "Thank you," or "I appreciate you," or "Great job!" Oh sure, I think it. But, as near as I can tell, the people around me and around you have not yet mastered the art of mind-reading. So tell them! Building up your gratitude muscles doesn't take much time. But it does take intention.

Are You Living in "Fantasyland"?

L iving in Central Florida, the home of Disney World and Universal Studios, I am very familiar with the fun, fame, and fortune that gets created by fantasy. Whether it's the new Star Wars, Galaxy's Edge theme that just opened at the Disney parks, or any number of "escape rooms" that seem to be popping up everywhere, people love their fantasies.

But there is another kind of fantasy that exists that's not so fun and probably even more prevalent. This kind of fantasy doesn't lead to fame, fortune, or fun. No, it breeds another F-word—FEAR.

For example, right now as I write this letter, I am bracing for hurricane Dorian to either impact or skirt the east coast of Florida. It's been on the news non-stop for days now. While the actual weather outside is calm, the weather inside my mind and heart is all stirred up. What if we take a direct hit? Will any of the large trees that surround my house come crashing into my living room? I remember Hurricane Charley that hit us back in 2004.

We lost power for days, spent weeks cutting up fallen trees, and waited months before FEMA was able to haul off the downed logs and limbs that lined our street. I don't want to go through something like that ever again.

I'm all keyed up, anxious, and worried about what might happen. But what might happen is a fantasy. It's just my mind playing out a fearful scenario. It's a kind of fantasy—just a future outcome I am imagining. The good news is that you and I have a choice about the things we fantasize about. If I don't want to dwell on the possibility of anticipating what might happen, I can choose to change my mental channel. I can set my mind on something else.

So if you find yourself being anxious, worrying about a future outcome that might happen, change your mental channel. Maybe you imagine a relationship breakup, a business downturn, a worst-case health diagnosis. Decide to imagine a different scenario—better yet, do something proactive now to help you prepare for the worst-case scenario. Often when you take active steps to prepare for the worst, it makes it easier for you to be less anxious about the future and stop losing your joy over the fantasy of what might happen—but might not!

Life is too short, too precious, to spend hours, days, even years in the fantasy that leads to fear. It can be a challenge at first—far too often we've gotten used to just assuming the worst-case outcome. Let's develop the ability to be more present in the moment, and when necessary do the things today that will help you best manage the circumstances of what may happen tomorrow. You will find yourself spending less time living in fear and have more confidence about your future.

Let's Put Things into Perspective

January, 2021—We were a week into a new year and the coronavirus was still with us. While vaccines were being distributed confirmed cases were continuing to rise in most parts of the country. At the same time, we were watching our nation's Capitol being stormed and our country felt more divided in terms of political philosophies than any of us could recall. It was easy to think the sky was falling.

But my friend and social media guru Leilani Haywood had recently written something about perspective that I thought was worthy to share with you then as well as now. Here's a summary of what she said:

"I started off the new year in tears as I considered several friends who died in 2020 due to Covid-19. And then I watch the news and see all the social and political unrest. It was disheartening. But then I was reminded of what life was like for my mom, my grandmother, and my great grandmother....

"For Mom, it was the Vietnam War and the end of WWII. For my grandmother, it was two world wars and the Great Depression. For my great-great-grandmother, it was probably the occupation of the Spanish in the Philippines on my father's side or the influx of foreigners into the Hawaiian Islands.

"I forget that every generation has had chaos, wars, famine, and disaster. What I choose to do in a time when protestors are breaking into the nation's Capitol is to look at how far we have come.

"We have a long way to go but I haven't had to deal with a world war in my lifetime—and I hope I never have to. I haven't left my country and my family for a better life like my grandparents did when they left the Philippines in the early 1900s. I haven't jumped on a ship fleeing for a better life in a foreign country like my grandfather on my mother's side.

"The point is we have it good. I have lived in the same house for over twenty years married to the same man for almost thirty years. Stability, love, and care is my base camp. So today, and going forward, I choose to look to the good. To fix in my mind the things that are right."

I thought Leilani's words were worth sharing with you as we journey together into the unknown adventures that await us.

When Comparing Corrupts

Yesterday I found myself trolling a competitor's website. They started in business about the same time I launched HigherLife. I made note of several things I thought they were doing very well, perhaps better than us. It motivated me to push forward, not settle, and strive to be better.

OK. If I just stopped there we would have a happy ending to the story. Unfortunately most of us don't. We buy a new stereo, marry the person of our dreams, land that ideal job, and after a while, instead of celebrating what we have, we start to compare with what somebody else has. Somebody's wife is more affectionate, somebody has a nicer lawn, their stereo puts out more bass, their car has a cooler emblem on the trunk lid. That comparison doesn't fuel our hunger to improve, it makes us itchy for change. We become disgruntled, discontent. We lose our joy. We second guess our choices. What's wrong with us?

For me life is a constant ping-pong toss between being content, satisfied with who I am and what I have and striving to be better, to achieve and to embrace the best version of me possible. Can you relate? In life as well as in business it's important to recognize the difference between settling and striving. Learn to be content with who you are and where you are in life, and yet don't get so comfortable with the status quo that you become complacent and settle for less than what's possible. It takes wisdom to recognize the gifts you have (including your imperfections) that should be embraced and the habits and circumstances that are worth jettisoning for something better.

The Six Fundamentals of Leadership

recently read an article in the Harvard Business Review by Ron Ashkenas and Brook Manville titled, "The Fundamentals of Leadership Still Haven't Changed." I thought the article had merit, so I want to share my summary take-away with you. Essentially the article shared that while a multitude of books on leadership have been written and someone is always coming out with the latest and greatest innovation in the area of leadership, true leadership still comes down to six areas of competency.

Understand that leaders must be proficient in the specific areas where they serve. I can't lead a publishing and marketing company well if I don't know much about publishing or marketing. Many leadership roles require unique experience and skillsets. Leading the team at SpaceX would be difficult if you didn't know anything about rockets. However, the following competencies are timeless and universal and I believe they have application for leading well whether you pastor a church or police a dog park. When you consider yourself as a leader, how do you stack up?

1. Uniting people around an exciting, aspirational vision;

2. Building a strategy for achieving the vision by making choices about what to do and what not to do;

3. Attracting and developing the best possible talent to implement the strategy;

4. Relentlessly **focusing on results** in the context of the strategy;

5. Creating **ongoing innovation** that will help renew or even reinvent the vision and strategy;

and

6. "Leading yourself": knowing and growing yourself so that you can most effectively lead others and carry out these practices.

Consider creating a simple graph with these six key characteristics and then rating yourself as well as your leadership team. Better yet, why not ask your team to rate you in these areas?

What are ways you can invest in your own leadership growth to expand and improve in each of these areas? Where are you the most competent and strong? Where perhaps do you struggle more as a leader? Why not take time to step back and evaluate your own performance as a leader and take steps to implement plans to inspire growth in each of these fundamental leadership areas?

Double Vision

I wear glasses—well I should say I HAVE glasses. I don't wear them all that often. My lenses correct for two different things, reading up close and seeing things clearly at a distance. But when it comes to interacting with people, there are two different views, two different perspectives we need to have.

This is a kind of "double vision" that gifted leaders have. They can spot latent talent. They see what a person can do, given the right opportunity and motivation—who they can become. Most of us are too quick to assess, to judge a person based solely on where they are in the present moment. It is a wonderful thing to be able to recognize human potential and create those moments of opportunity where a person, if properly challenged, can rise. Smart leaders can see gifts, talents, and possibility in someone else that perhaps they can't see in themselves.

To be sure, this is a delicate dance, being able to accept a person where they are with all their flaws, failures, insecurities, and idiosyncrasies, and at the same time recognize all that they could be. If you ever watch any of the home remodeling shows on HGTV, you see how the designers look at a house that has lost its curb appeal, that is dated in its layout. But they see what's possible. Even before a blueprint of the remodeling job is drafted, they can see in their mind's eye what that house could become with the right modifications.

Well, if a house or a car or a piece of furniture can be revived into something more useful, functional, and pleasing in its design, how much greater a gift it is to be a person who can both accept others for where they are and at the same time, see their potential. Better yet, invest time and effort in bringing out that potential in others.

So in your daily interaction with people, let me challenge you to look past how a person may be acting or reacting to you right now and see them for what they can be. This requires a level of vulnerability. You run the risk of being disappointed. Just because you see the potential someone else has, doesn't mean they will agree with you or pursue that potential for themselves. But you can do your part. You be the person who recognizes their potential and do all that you can to call that forth. Create the opportunity for someone else to rise and step into their higher potential. Not everyone will respond to what you see. That's OK. You be the person who is known for both accepting people where they are and at the same time encouraging, challenging, and creating opportunity for them to become something more.

Do this and you will live a life that others want to emulate and be around. Your sphere of influence will expand as you make those around you better. That is true leadership!

Where Are Your Faucets Leaking?

I often comment that I feel like the plumber whose own faucets are leaking. I regularly consult, coach, and encourage clients on best practices for how they can build their audiences, enhance their brand, generate revenue, and bring value to the people they most want to serve. I'm good at envisioning for others how they can spin their talent, know-how, and experience into impactful strands of gold.

When it comes to taking my own advice and doing the things that I know would be most beneficial in connecting with the customers we want to serve through HigherLife, well let's just say, I'm not what you'd call my "ideal client." Why is it we so often don't do the very things we need to do? Or keep doing the things we know are not productive or helpful? Allow me to offer four thoughts on this. Let me know to which, if any, of these four growth-stoppers and vision-inhibitors you fall prey. . . .

> **1. Force of habit**—As the group Chicago sang a few decades ago, "You're a Hard Habit to

Break." Where have you fallen into a routine that's become an unhealthy habit? What choice can you make today to break that habit?

2. No plan—If you want to change a behavior pattern that's not productive, whether it's deciding to eat less, exercise more, stop writing so many emails, start writing that book you've said you need to write, whatever behavior you need to change, you need a plan!

3. You're emotionally drained—If you are too busy, or overworked, you will be far less likely to have the emotional energy it takes to break your habit or make your plan. So find the time in your day or week when your energy level is up, your motivation is high. This is the better time to initiate your plan to think and act differently.

4. Have some accountability—Nothing ever changes in an environment of ambiguity. If you need to get something done or change a behavior you've got to have some accountability. Have someone you trust follow up with you. Give yourself specific, measurable deadlines and hold yourself to them. If necessary, insert consequences for failing to keep to your plan.

Let's be honest, we all have some "leaky faucets" in our lives, those places where we need to improve, where we know what to do, and we just need help with the execution. Great intentions are meaningless. It's all about the execution! No need to call a plumber—you can work on this yourself!

Giving Honor

The other day I was having a conversation with a friend, a young woman I've only known and worked with for a short while. We were talking about someone we both know and neither one of us particularly likes. This person has a pretty high position in an organization my friend does volunteer work for. I was enjoying (probably a little too much) complaining about this person we both know.

But then my friend said something that surprised and challenged me. She said, "While I don't care for——, I realize that he is above me and I need to give him the honor he is due." Wow. That statement caught me off guard. But I knew she was right. I was not only complaining about another human being, I was trying to pull my friend in on my rant-fest as well. She was wise enough to cut me off.

Extending honor to others is not something we talk about all that often. In truth, it's much easier (and perhaps initially more satisfying) to grumble, to whine or to complain about another person's faults and shortcomings.

What would happen if we were more intentional in giving honor to someone, even when they irritate us, or we feel they don't deserve it? What if we extended them honor just because it's the right thing to do? Just because their position in your company warrants that honor?

Could it be that when you give someone honor, they more easily begin to act in a manner that aligns with the honor you are giving? Maybe you are not being as coy or clever in hiding your disdain for a co-worker as you think you are. People can sense when they are not appreciated, valued, or respected. So when you start to extend honor to another person, especially when you don't feel like it, perhaps that sets in motion a positive chain reaction that will help the person blossom and mature. Try reviling less and revering more. Give honor where honor is due.

The Strength of Comfort

Everybody wants to be comfortable, right? In some ways, we have exchanged the "American Dream" of life, liberty, and the pursuit of happiness for it. We work hard to rid our lives of all stressors, influences that would rob us of being comfortable.

When we think of comfort, we think of things being at ease, of life being cushy and easy. But I recently discovered that "comfort" is actually something quite different. Comfort means "to give strength." The verb comfort comes from the Latin word *comfortare*, which means "strengthen greatly." So to comfort someone means to fortify them, to enable them to be strengthened in the midst of their struggle or pain. To experience comfort is not so much about removing all the obstacles in your life but rather being strengthened in the midst of them.

So is taking that extra night course in order to better yourself, that pushing yourself to go the extra mile to improve your job performance or make your company better, that hitting the gym at six in the morning to stay in good shape making you more comfortable? The answer is yes! The things that you do to strengthen your life, to fortify yourself for the future, are indeed increasing your comfort.

I don't know about you, but I need to change my thinking. Now, when someone says to me, "Don't get too comfortable," my response will be, "Why not?" Now, I won't think about sacrificing my drive to better myself, to achieve and succeed on the altar of comfort. Rather, I will apply myself to gaining the strength I need to withstand disappointment, economic downturns, and unplanned peril, the stuff that comes to all of us at one time or another. I will seek to "gain strength" knowing that strength is causing deep roots to be grown in my life. That way, when the winds of life blow, I will withstand them. I will be comfortable.

How about you? Where can you give strength to someone else? What can you do this week that will strengthen your body, your mind, your spirit to become a more resilient, capable, and loving person? Let's increase our comfort!

If You're Not Yet Awesome—Try This

I was on my way home from a first meeting with a prospective client. The meeting went very well, so much so that my appointment wrote me a check on the spot, before I had even sent them a contract. I don't think that's ever happened to me. I called Michelle, my operations director, to share the good news. She said, "You must be getting awesome at prospecting." I responded, "I may not be awesome, but when it comes to prospecting, I'm definitely more disciplined than I've ever been." (If you've read my writing for any length of time, you know that prospecting for new business is not something I enjoy doing.) That's it! Even as I responded to Michelle, those words struck me. When you aren't naturally gifted at something—you haven't arrived at "awesome status"—diligence and discipline will often more than compensate. In fact, the disciplined person who maybe isn't as naturally gifted at something will often outperform the one who has the natural talent but has not married that talent or ability with discipline.

Being disciplined is an essential character trait. Maybe it's not the first thing you think of, such as being thoughtful, kind, loving, generous, forgiving, or considerate. But being a person who can exercise self-discipline in any area of life will benefit you in countless ways. And if you can be disciplined in one area of your life, whether it's watching what you eat, what you watch on TV, how you speak, how you study, that means you can be disciplined in any area of your life.

We discipline our children, not because we want to punish them but because you don't become disciplined without experiencing discipline. Discipline is a gift. It's a commitment and often a conscientious act of love. Being disciplined and having discipline will make you a better person. It's a character trait that will serve you well, especially in the many areas of life where you may be required to perform or to act that are not aligned with your natural strengths. Let's face it, we don't get to pick and choose everything that we have to put our hands to. We all have to do stuff that we're not good at or that we don't enjoy. And when that happens, have the discipline to apply yourself well. If you do—you will be on your way to being awesome!

Things That Are Priceless

My wife loves to work on scrapbooks. She's spent the better part of recent summer months working to update the scrapbooks for each of our three grown sons. From time to time I wander into her back office, which these days is our enclosed back porch. I flip through the pages and a lifetime of memories come flooding back—the photos in those books remind me of family vacations, milestone events, the different stages of our lives as we were raising a family, as well as the simple, silly memories of the crazy things we all do—holiday traditions, family traditions, all forming a tapestry that shapes our values, our priorities, even our worldview.

Over the Labor Day weekend I joined some of my grand-kids sliding down a large, blow-up water slide that was erected in our son and daughter-in-law's back yard. It was a Saturday afternoon filled with fun and laughter. When I wasn't being the "crazy grandpa" on the slide, I would sit in a lawn chair just watching the little ones laughing, playing and wrestling with their dad to determine who could remain at the top of the slide the longest without getting pushed out and down the slide. A modified version of "King of the Mountain." This got me thinking ... that time just hanging out with family, doing nothing of consequence other than having fun together is probably making really wonderful memories not just for me, but for my kids and their kids. How do you put a price on that?

You work so hard, focusing on managing and growing your business, taking care of all the responsibilities that life requires—the things you need to do to pay the bills, to get ahead, to provide security, to be responsible, to check things off your to-do list. And yet, the time you invest with your family to keep relationships strong or perhaps to mend or heal a relationship that has been frayed—these are the things you simply can't measure in dollars and cents or in time increments. They are priceless.

So my encouragement for you today is simply this. Take time to think about where this week you can invest in something priceless ... something that won't show up on a spreadsheet or balance sheet. Invest in a relationship with a loved one—or perhaps someone you are mentoring. Make sure you make some truly priceless contributions each and every week. That's a recipe for a marvelous life!

From Setback to Slingshot

If you've ever built a model catapult or trebuchet for one of your kid's school projects, you understand the principle of pulling a large object backwards in order to fling it forwards. Pitchers do it all the time. The wind-up precedes the throw. So it is in life. We get hit with setbacks, problems, unexpected challenges that put us back on our heels emotionally, financially, relationally, sometimes physically.

What do you do?

The wise person looks for ways to convert the negative energy of the current crisis into the positive momentum that will hurl them forward.

OK, give yourself a few minutes to commiserate over your setback. Whine, fuss, complain—but only for a moment. Don't stay there. Instead, look for the opportunity to advance, to learn, to grow, to slingshot your circumstances forward. Bad things happen to good people ... no wait, bad things happen to ALL people. It's inescapable. But what makes the difference between being a casualty or a conqueror is often the outlook, the perspective you choose to embrace. That's right. Your attitude and outlook is a choice. You have the power within you to change your perspective.

Our nation is reeling from the one-two punch of a pandemic and racial unrest. You may be facing a financial crisis, a health crisis, or something else. Allow me to be the cheerleader in your corner that whispers, "You can do this! You were made for this moment. Your hour of greatness, of discovery, of revelation, and success is upon you."

I was speaking with a friend yesterday who was telling me of his need to make more money. He has a great and satisfying job—one that's quite comfortable. But his circumstances are now compelling him to launch a new business. He shared the idea with me. As he was talking, I was smiling on the inside. Why? Because I could see his future perhaps even before he could. I could see my friend helping more people, earning more income, and enjoying more personal fulfillment than his comfortable job affords him. He is needing to take a step back in order to experience the slingshot momentum of his future success.

So how about you? What setback are you facing that can be the catalyst to move you into your desired destiny? Change your mind. Change your thinking. Change your words. Change your actions. Change your results!

I Think We've Got It Backwards

How often do you charge into your day, your week, your month, full-steam-ahead and then work to fit in some necessary down time to recharge your emotional, intellectual, and physical batteries? It's the American way, right? Work hard and recharge—rinse and repeat! But recently I heard a sermon that got me thinking perhaps we have it backwards. Instead of plowing forward, head down, pedal-to-the-metal all day and then coming up for air, taking a needed break, maybe we need to reverse things. Maybe our bodies work best when we focus on getting the rest we need first and then charge forward from that place of being fully energized.

Think about it. When does your day start? At seven a.m.? Eight a.m.? No, your day started at midnight. That's when a new day begins. What are you doing at midnight? Hopefully, sleeping—resting, giving your body and your mind the rest they need to be productive, to function at a peak level.

In the Bible, the first chapter of Genesis, where we read about God's creative activity in creating the known physical world, each day is not described as morning and evening, but rather evening and then morning. Each day started with what we think of as the resting period, evening, followed by the activity period, morning.

So as you think of ways to maximize your productivity and your creativity, instead of planning out all that you have to do and then figuring out how to fit in some rest time, flip that scenario. Plan your rest first and then schedule your day to follow.

Perhaps you have seen the illustration of trying to fit marbles and sand into a glass jar. If you pour in the sand first, there is not enough room in the jar to hold all the marbles. But if you fill your jar with the marbles first, then pour in the sand, that sand can fill in all the spaces around the marbles and both fit nicely into the jar container. It's all about priorities—what you put into the jar first.

Schedule your rest first, and see if your working hours don't become more energetic and productive.

A Formula for Success

E veryone wants to be successful. Books are written about it. People attend seminars to discover the secret to success. Philosophers pontificate on the meaning of success. How do you define success?

Well, my brother recently sent me an email (you may have seen a variation of this yourself), that quantified success in simple mathematical terms. Being more of a wordsmith than a mathematician, I thought it might be a fun change of pace to share this simple formula with you.

Here it is....

Everyone talks about giving 100%, achieving 100%. It's not uncommon to hear people say they're giving more than 100%, as if that's possible. Can you achieve 110%? Can you be 107% successful? But I digress. Let's stick to the premise that being 100% successful in life, in your work, in your relationships, is the goal and it's actually achievable. What's the secret? How do you get there?

Well here you go.... It's a mathematical formula that might help you answer these questions.

If:

A B C D E F G H I J K L M N O P Q R S T U V
W X Y Z

Is represented as:

1 2 3 4 5 6 7 8 9 10 11 12 13 14 15 16 17 18 19
20 21 22 23 24 25 26

Then:

H-A-R-D-W-O-R-K

$8+1+18+4+23+15+18+11 = 98\%$

And:

K-N-O-W-L-E-D-G-E

$11+14+15+23+12+5+4+7+5 = 96\%$

But:

A-T-T-I-T-U-D-E

$1+20+20+9+20+21+4+5 = 100\%$

Success starts on the inside and works its way out. How you think directs how you live. The great thing about attitude is that it is completely within your control. You can't control the weather. You can't control what happens to you or the circumstances of life. We all get dealt bad hands and good hands. But one thing you can control is your attitude, how you respond to the things that come your way.

So this week, no matter how great or stressful or frightening or overwhelming or how wonderful your life circumstances may be, make the choice to live 100%. It starts with your attitude.

Blind Spots

Blind spots. We all have them. Here's the problem with a blind spot ... you don't see it! It's the nature of a blind spot. If you could see it, it wouldn't be a blind spot, would it? So how do you become aware of and work through a blind spot?

I know one of my blind spots is that I sometimes come across more aggressive, more intense than I intend. In my head I think I'm being easy-going and calm, totally reasonable in my request. What I've learned is that what comes out of my mouth is not always received that way. My intensity and passion can be received as accusatory or caustic. I think I am motivating but in truth I might be intimidating or overwhelming. Do I see this? Not in the moment. It's a blind spot for me.

So how do you become aware of your blind spots? Just as important, how do you fix them? For starters one way is to surround yourself with people who are close enough to you, who care about you enough that they will tell you. You can make it easier to receive constructive criticism by regularly asking for it. Create a culture of candor, of honesty, openness, and vulnerability so that the people who work with and for you are willing to stick their neck out to help you.

When they do, you need to resist the natural temptation to snap back, to deny or to justify your actions. Make a point to not say anything—just listen. Only when your friend, family member, or associate has finished talking can you take a deep breath, say thank you, and then commit to do the necessary internal work and soul-searching to see if their points are valid. If so, be willing to ask for advice on what you can do about your blind spot. This is how you get better. It's how you can grow as a professional, as a parent, as a person!

Let's face it, we are all a "work in progress." Beating yourself up over your shortcomings, your blind spots, is a waste of time. It won't make you feel any better and certainly won't help you more quickly embrace the changes that need to be made. (Guilt and shame never do.) So be the kind of person who is willing to look honestly at yourself—and like what you see! Know that discovering and dealing with your blind spots, no matter how ugly or disappointing they may be, is going to help you be a better person.

Take comfort in knowing that there is a glorious version of you in process, waiting to be revealed!

A Farmer's Guide to Investing and Success

recently attended a Home Owners Association meeting for where I live. Among the items on the agenda we talked about how the trees in our neighborhood play a significant role in making our community both distinctive and desirable. As more mature trees become damaged or diseased, people want to remove them to avoid the hazard of a huge tree falling during a windstorm or hurricane.

I made the comment that if we want to preserve the character of our wooded neighborhood, we need to be planting new trees as we take older ones down. There are massive trees that overhang my driveway that I remember when they were planted almost thirty years ago.

What every farmer understands is that if you want a rich harvest tomorrow you have to sow seeds today. If you want mature trees, you have to invest in planting young ones. If you want seasoned leadership on your team, you have to invest in raw talent. If you want more clients tomorrow, you have to plant a lot of prospecting today.

Big businesses understand this. But it's easier for them to look farther ahead and invest in the long-term success. The process of finding, drilling, and refining crude oil can take ten to fifteen years easy. The time to research, discover, do clinical trials to bring a new drug to market is about the same. But these large companies typically have the market share and the capital to take that longer view of investing for success.

What about the small business owner, the solopreneur, the professional consultant or coach who doesn't have the means to wait several years for their business to develop? We should learn from our farmer friends who sow to harvest a future crop while tending and tilling a present crop. We must not get so caught up in managing the present that we fail to lead into our future.

Take some time this week to consider where you want to be five, maybe ten years from now. Ask yourself what seeds, what investment can you make this month that will put you in position to see your five to ten year vision come to pass.

To your coming harvest....

Embrace the Pain

I don't like it one bit. But the tough truth is, humans were made to suffer and endure hardship. Take away the pain, the challenge, the struggle and we don't thrive, we die.

You see it throughout nature—the butterfly entombed in its cocoon gains strength to fly through its struggle to escape. The couple that loses a child forms a charity, raising millions to help others who face a similar journey. The young man from the projects who excels in sport motivated in part through his pain and desire to escape it. Both clay and steel are hardened through fire.

As parents we go to any length to spare our kids pain, sorrow, disappointment, and hurt. It's natural. And yet behind almost every great story resides a struggle. Did you know there are five core elements of every story: PLOT, CHARACTER, SETTING, THEME and CONFLICT. Within the conflict lies the pain and suffering. Every romantic comedy you read or watch follows the pattern: boy meets girl, falls for girl, breaks up with the girl and gets back together to live happily ever after.

Take away the breakup section, remove the conflict and the story is, well, boring.

We simply cannot avoid pain and suffering, no matter how hard we try. We all face difficulty and struggle, and we know that the struggle, no matter how desperate and horrid, has the potential to make us better and to bring about some form of good. So let's purpose to look for the good, pursue it, speak about it, hope for it, no matter whether you are just entering a season of strife, mired in the thick of it, or finally coming out of it. Smile. You can do this ... you are incredibly resilient. This will make you better.

Putting Lipstick on a Pig

T he other day I was on my way to a meeting and noticed a rather average-looking grey Honda. I think it was a Civic. The car's paint was faded and it was probably fifteen years old. What caught my attention and caused me to smile is I noted the car probably had $3,500 worth of custom accessories on it—custom wheels (pink, I might add), low profile tires, tuned exhaust. The accessories I'm sure were worth more than the whole car.

It reminded me of the phrase "putting lipstick on a pig," which got me thinking. How many places are we doing the same thing with our businesses? We are spending time and money trying to "dress up" worn out marketing strategies that just aren't performing like they used to. They're old. They're tired. Maybe it's like that with your hiring practices, or even the way you make strategic business decisions.

We are creatures of habit. And when we get overworked or overwhelmed we stop thinking creatively, objectively, and strategically. We default to what's familiar and convenient, even if it's outdated or has lost its effectiveness.

So my challenge to you is this. Take some time to think about each area of your work or ministry. Identify one process or program that looks like a pig—something you need to let go of rather than continue to dress up.

And may you have a stylish day!

Whose Burdens Do You Carry?

The other day I read a book by David Gregory that challenged me to consider all the things that I do that are not really my responsibility; they're God's. (I'd provide you a link to order the book but it's not yet available.) As a person of faith, this is an easy thing to do ... feel the need to make the world better, or maybe just make my own life better by "playing God." There's a difference between making yourself available to allow God to work through you and you attempting to do what only God can do.

Do you struggle with picking up tasks, carrying burdens that are not yours to bear? It's a common problem that a lot of us have.

This idea of picking up what's not yours to do shows up in our work life as well. I can be rather anal about certain details on how I want our business to run, how we treat our clients. While my passion for excellence may be admirable, the downside is that I often take back tasks that have already been delegated. Instead of allowing people to figure things out on their own, maybe even fail, I step in. I pick up responsibility that is not mine to carry.

Picking up what's not yours to carry creeps into relationships as well as work. For example, I learned many years ago that it's never wise to pick up someone else's offense. You know, your friend Robert ticks off your friend Sarah or hurts her feelings. Not only is Sarah offended with Rob, now you are too. But why? How does picking up Sarah's offense in any way solve a problem or bring value to your life, Sarah's life, or Robert's life?

So take a moment to take an internal inventory and ask yourself where perhaps you are carrying a burden, taking on a task or a responsibility that is not yours to carry, that belongs with someone else.

May you spend the precious time you have been gifted today doing exactly what you are supposed to be doing and pay attention to the things that only you are called to do.

Don't Get Comfortable with Mediocrity

When you purchase a new car, you probably pay attention to where you park, at least for awhile, in order to avoid getting a door ding—OK, maybe this is just my issue. But I'm a "car guy" so the thought of having a ding in the smooth side of a new ride just drives me crazy. (I admit this may be a short drive.)

But once you get that first ding, and then another, over time it bothers you less and less. Same with any home spruce-up you do. Right after you have the windows washed, you are attentive to cleaning up the smudges. After you put a fresh coat of paint on the walls, you notice when the walls get smudged or dinged. But after awhile those smudges, dings, and imperfections simply don't bother you anymore—at least not enough to do anything about it.

When it comes to your work habits, your leadership, your thought life, are there some areas that need to be addressed— that initially bothered you but over time, you've gotten used to them and now you just let it slide?

It takes wisdom to know what things are "good enough" and not worth obsessing over and where perhaps we have allowed a habit, an attitude, a flaw in our work methodology or worse, our character, to remain undealt with. This is how mediocrity sets in. We settle. We get comfortable with the status quo. Listen, just because nobody is actively complaining about something doesn't mean it's to your profit to allow that area of mediocrity to remain. People who get ahead in life tend to be those who push themselves, who don't settle, and who set a higher bar of personal performance. They don't get comfortable with their flaws and shortcomings but instead they work on them.

So my challenge for you today is to take a moment to consider where perhaps you've gotten comfortable with mediocrity. Where have you settled for less than what's best? If you can identify just one thing, one area, and make the conscious decision to work on that area, to set a new expectation, a new standard for yourself, that will be wonderful. Maybe you are habitually five minutes late for meetings and appointments. You've gotten comfortable with that expectation. That's a ding, an area of mediocrity that you can choose to improve. Nobody has been complaining, but you have no idea what people mutter about you behind your back. Maybe you don't shave as often as you should or you tend to repeat a phrase ("you know?" or "like") over and over. It's not the end of the world—just annoying and it's a ding on your communications skills. Take a step back and look for an area of mediocrity, a ding, that you can work on. This is how you rise, you achieve, you become better, one good decision, one upgrade at a time!

Planting Seeds

Are you planting seeds of trees under whose boughs you will never sit? I learned this phrase many years ago from a leader I respect named Bill Wilson. Bill founded and heads a ministry to street kids based out of Brooklyn New York called Metro World Child. The phrase has stuck with me over the years and it's a powerful reminder to make sure I am investing my time, talent, and treasure in things that count.

We live in an increasingly short-term culture. Here today, gone tomorrow. Today's latest fad and hottest gadget will be obsolete, an archaic dinosaur, not just in a matter of decades but literally in months!

Yet, despite the pace of change and innovation that can sometimes lead to emotional hyperventilation, you can choose to invest in some things that have staying power, that will outlive you. Their impact and influence will live on, long after you're dead and gone. What am I talking about? People!

I spend a good part of my day thinking about and working on process; how to do things better, more effectively, and efficiently. What tools can I use that will increase profit margin or the level of customer service we offer? To be sure, these things are valuable. But I want to make sure that I am also investing in things that lead to significance, to influence and impact, not just to short-term success.

How about you? As you evaluate your time this week, this month and perhaps this year, take some time to step back and analyze where you are investing in people. In whose life are you pouring encouragement, hope, belief, courage, values, and character? I am so grateful to the people throughout my life, beginning with my parents, who invested in me. Any fruit that my life produces is a result, in part, of those who poured into me.

The neat thing is, there is never a season (hopefully) where this investment in others has to stop. I am still benefiting from what others, including those much younger than me, are investing into my life.

So go sow some good seed today!

What Drives You and Me?

The other day I was having lunch with a good friend, Dr. Joseph Thompson, and we got on the subject of the things that motivate us to change. Is it **external environment or internal empowerment?** Clearly both play a role in the decisions and choices we make.

However, it seems to me that we spend perhaps too much time (and money) trying to create the ideal external environment that will lead potential customers to engage with us, and perhaps not enough on impacting the internal empowerment. For example, if you run a car dealership and you want to get more people into your showroom, you can rent those air-filled giant flopping men to draw people in. You can offer special 4th of July savings, manufacturers rebates, and the list goes on and on. But what motivates me to make a decision that will cost me $10,000, $40,000, $70,000 or more? It's going to be the internal motivations of what I think I deserve—how great I will FEEL when I'm seen driving this new vehicle. At what point will my hunger, my desire for that new car outweigh the fear that I may be making a wrong decision, or just my fear of making any decision at all? We all know that emotion sells. That emotion may be externally stimulated but it is internally generated! Are there practical issues at stake? Of course, your current vehicle may be costing you more in repairs and Uber fares than what it will cost to finance a new vehicle. But recognize that once you decide THAT you need a car, the question of WHICH car will involve more of these powerful internal motivators.

So whether you are asking someone to make a donation to your charity, church, or cause; whether you are asking people to hire you as a coach, consultant, or speaker; whether you are selling a product or offering a service, ask yourself, what is the dominant internal driver that would cause someone to say yes to what you have to offer? What's the signature fear or inhibitor that is keeping them from saying yes?

Get together with others and brainstorm your answers to these questions. I'm going to be doing the same. Better yet, get with some of your customers as well as prospects who have not yet committed to working with you. Ask them these questions. Your answers may give you some powerful cues on how you can better present the value that you bring to the table.

Quality without Compromise

Recently I read this quote from business icon and philanthropist Warren Buffett:

> "It's far better to buy a wonderful company at a fair price than a fair company at a wonderful price."

Great advice. How often do we look for the "deal" only to discover that after the initial euphoria of feeling like we got a bargain, we are left with a product or service that is well, just not quite what we had hoped it would be. Don't get me wrong, I LOVE to negotiate and feel like I saved myself some money. But negotiating to get a lower price on exactly the product or service that you want is not the same thing as compromising what you want to get a lower price.

As I look back over my life, I realize that the "things" I treasure most are the ones of the highest value. Probably twenty-five years ago, I needed a briefcase. I really wanted a Hartman bag. To me, their style, color, and quality was everything I wanted. I just couldn't bring myself to spend what a Hartman bag cost which was five to ten times more than similarly styled bags I could find at a local discount or department store. I eventually found a Hartman Outlet store up in Maine, and bought a discontinued model. I paid half of what the bag cost retail but even then, it was still three times what I could have spent on a knock-off. But to this day I still have that bag, and I still love it.

The same goes for my acoustic guitar. It's a Taylor and while it was not cheap, it was exactly what I wanted and is likely the last guitar I will ever own. Every time I play it, I smile.

My point is, whether you are providing a product or service or buying one, go for the quality you want then negotiate your best price rather than going for the best price and pressing for higher quality. Things just work better that way.

I don't know how it is in your business, but invariably when our team tries to cut corners to get a price down to meet a client's budget, it almost always backfires. The client usually ends up pressing for the higher level of quality they wanted in the first place and either we cave and give it to them (they win, we lose) OR, we stand our ground and stick to the terms we agreed to, but the client doesn't get quite what they wanted (we win, they lose). The Win-Win space we both want is to establish the level of quality and service or product specification they really want, and then work to deliver that at the best possible price for the client.

May your words and your actions deliver quality today!

The Difference Your Words Make

The other day I was part of a symposium dealing with the need to "do church differently" in order to reach people who have become disenchanted or disillusioned with what they see as the traditional or institutional church organization. In the conversation I brought up the point that we can't properly address the format and structure of how church is done without addressing the language we use.

Think about it, people routinely think of church as a building, an organization, a type of service, a membership. Each of these connections is sadly lacking from the original intended meaning. Church was referenced in the Bible as a "body" and a "bride"—a living entity that is both complex and beautiful. Yet in today's culture, the meaning we so easily ascribe to the term is something inanimate, simplistic, and sadly not all that attractive. So to "do church differently" we need a new paradigm or at least a new language that means what we intend it to mean. If I am "progressive" does that mean I am a forward thinker or adhere to a liberal form of governing?

If I say that black lives matter, or blue lives matter, does that mean I favor some form of social inequality? Bottom line, what words mean to us may not translate as clearly as we think.

This got me thinking, in what ways are we limiting our own growth because we continue to use language that perhaps means one thing to us, but means something quite different to the people we most want to reach and serve? Where do we use words that have perhaps lost their meaning? If I say to my wife, "I love you," in the same sentence with "I love to play golf," am I communicating something to her I clearly did not intend?

How about for the next few weeks you focus on these three things:

> **1. Be More Positive than Critical**—The proportions you use can make all the difference. Combine flour, sugar, and water in one proportion and you get bread. In a different proportion you get a cookie. Identify a few people in your sphere of influence and make a point to change the proportions of your positive communication with your corrective and critical communication. See what happens.
>
> **2. Be More Specific than General**—Telling someone they look nice doesn't carry as much meaning as saying you notice their new hairstyle or the new shoes they are wearing or the way they handled a tough conversation with a co-worker.

3. Be More Inventive—Broaden your vocabulary by using adjectives and language that spark images and pictures. Instead of saying, "Having to write my last new product pitch was much harder than I thought," say something like, "Writing that proposal felt like I was trying to run the length of a football field in waist-deep water." Or, "I felt like I had to write a proposal on quantum physics using my fourth-grade science book."

Where Does Your Identity Hide?

In life there are constant demands on your time and attention. It's easy to get lost—to find yourself going through the motions. You are working hard, paddling as fast as you can, trying to keep your head above the waterline and not drown in your own to-do list. Along the way, perhaps you stop and ask yourself, "Who am I?" "Am I making a difference?" "Am I spending my time and energy on the right things, the things that will matter most not just in my own life, but for my family, for my future, and for eternity?"

I think one of the most helpful and healthy things you can do is periodically step back and make sure that you are spending your energy on things related to your purpose, your mission and your identity—which begs the question, "Where do you find your identity?"

My friend Jon Davis and I were having breakfast recently and he commented on something Tod Bolsinger shared in a meeting Jon was attending. Tod is the author of multiple books including *Canoeing the Mountains,* which is about leading in uncharted territory. According to Tod, the way you get at your mission is by discovering your identity and you find your identity in the stories you tell.

As someone who is invested in the power of "story," this statement resonated with me. Think about it, what are the stories you love to tell? What are the victories and conquests about which you are most proud? Chances are the things that you talk about, that you celebrate and share most often, are stories that connect with your identity, who you really are.

The stories you tell speak to your aspirations—who you desire to be. Maybe your nine to five is working construction but you long to be a singer, an entertainer. The stories that captivate you, the stories you share will more likely speak to your calling, your desire, than your current status.

Ideally who you are already lines up with what you do. But if not, maybe you need to consider realigning your time and your work so that they are more in sync with your identity. I suspect the more in alignment you are, the greater peace, contentment, and satisfaction you will experience.

I am a visionary, and I love to create—so I find myself gravitating to working with people who want to create something—a book for example. I also am an encourager; it's just part of my nature. If I take the DISC test, I am off the charts as a people person. So, the authors whose books I get most excited about are the ones that are all about building up others and encouraging. The stories I tell are often themed around people encounters more than tasks accomplished.

So how about you? How in touch, how aware are you of your own identity, your own story? Are you living out your best story? If so, great. If not, make plans to make some changes so that where you focus your time and talent is more aligned with your identity. Maybe you have a great job that pays well but is not aligned well with your identity. You have responsibilities and can't just quit and go look for something else. OK, but how about getting more involved as a volunteer with organizations whose work feeds your soul? Where can you invest your free time that will foster and support your identity—that will give you more stories that you will love to tell!

It's Easy to Say ...
But Hard to Do

In life it seems we are regularly plagued with two challenges ... knowing what to do and then mustering the courage, conviction, and will-power to follow through and do it.

I don't know about you but in running my business I can show you pages of brilliant strategy—outlines of passionate plans and awesome ideas that my team and I have come up with. And yet, as the saying goes, **"execution is everything."** Great ideas are a dime a dozen.... Following through on those great ideas, well that's something else.

So how can you be more intentional in staying on track, staying focused, and **actually following through** with the plans that you have so artfully prepared? I'd love to tell you there is a silver bullet, a secret sauce for this. There isn't. It's different for everybody. Here are some ideas that may be helpful to you in improving your follow-through.

Whether you are parenting your child or practicing your golf swing, it's the follow-through that matters.

1. Limit your options—I'm a creative person, so the thought of limiting anything is anathema to me. I love to dream and think outside the box. That's great—up to a point. For you to get good at follow-through, you must be willing to limit your options, cut your to-do list down to what's manageable. My former boss used to say all the time, "You can't manage what you can't measure and what you measure and monitor improves." I agree. Make sure your to-do list is realistic and doable.

2. Keep it in front of you—As a list maker, this one is easy for me. I make lists of everything. I can have a list of my lists ... but by writing down the things that are most important for you to accomplish and keeping those things in front of you, you're less likely to get distracted and pulled off course. Set your phone to send you reminders ... post them on your laptop or the bathroom mirror. The important thing is to have reminders, have cues in plain sight to help you stay on task and finish what you start.

3. Break it into chunks—How do you eat an elephant? One bite at a time. Whatever is your goal or objective, break it into manageable chunks. Not only will you find it motivating to cross things off your list as you accomplish them, by breaking the task down into smaller pieces, you are more likely to stay focused and follow through to completion. When coaching authors about writing a book, I always encourage outlining the chapters first and then setting up a writing schedule to do one chapter at a time. Writing a 1,500-word chapter is a piece of cake, a couple hours of work, compared to writing a whole book. Give yourself a series of shorter assignments rather than one gargantuan task.

So what works for you? The important thing is that you set yourself up for success by making the choice to follow-through with whatever priorities you set. This applies in relationship as well as business. Did you promise to meet your spouse or significant other at a certain time for a date? Or show up at your friend's birthday party at a certain time? Keeping your word and following through will build trust and strengthen any relationship just as surely as failing to follow through will damage it.

So make a short list of things that are important for you to follow through on this week.

Now go be the best version of you possible.

The Importance of the "Other Side"

O ur world functions largely because of the power of "opposing forces." In physics—an airplane can fly largely because of how wind resistance flows over its wings. It's why airplanes take off and land best facing into the wind rather than with it.

We see it in nature. In Yellowstone National park, the reintroduction of wolves resulted in a massive regeneration of the ecosystem. Of course we see it in relationships—men are from Mars and women are from Venus—at least according to John Gray. Why is it that some of the healthiest marriages are where the man and the woman are wired completely different? You've heard the phrase, "opposites attract."

In mechanics, most things work in tension. The force of one engine piston pushing down forces the other piston up. As a result, the crankshaft turns. In sports, the speed of a baseball thrown in one direction enables the batter to smack it over the outfield wall for a homerun.

In organizations, leaders need to build a supportive team around them—people who share the leader's vision and who bring complimentary skill sets to the leader's gifting. Yet, if everyone on the team begins to run in lockstep together, if there are no contrarian voices, nobody to challenge the status quo, that can be a problem.

To be sure, all leaders need to be encouraged and supported. But the wise leader also recognizes the value of having people on the team who push back, who question, who think differently. Leaders need people willing to have the tough conversations, who slow things down enough so that more thoughtful evaluation of a project or direction can be considered. Often the best solution comes only after being forced to think outside the box, to consider alternatives that frankly wouldn't be brought up if everyone just went along with the leader's thinking. Insecure leaders who surround themselves with "yes-men" often become short-sighted and miss out on incredible opportunities in the name of avoiding thoughtful discussion, doing more research, and avoiding conflict.

Maybe you are that voice that's been silenced or pushed aside. Or maybe you are that leader who has been too quick to avoid meeting with someone who aggravates you just because they seem to challenge or question what everyone else seems to be on board with doing. I've been in board situations where I've been the only "no" vote. It's not fun. But sometimes it's necessary.

So consider who on your advisory team has the potential to help you see things from a new perspective. Who can artfully and with respect help you see the "other side" of a decision or direction? Value them and invite them into the decision-making process. You will be glad you did!

How to Win (or Lose) Before You Start

The other day I was reading a blog from best-selling author and strategist, Seth Godin. He was saying that in juggling, the key to success is not in the catch but rather the toss. Throwing is more important than catching. If you learn to throw the ball up properly, the catch tends to take care of itself.

This principle applies not just in juggling but in business and in life. You've heard the adage, "An ounce of prevention is worth a pound of cure." Think about how much time (and money) we spend repairing broken systems and broken relationships, that could have been avoided had we invested more time and effort in those systems and relationships BEFORE something went awry. Instead, our scramble to "catch" balls that have gone off course could be avoided had we put more effort into the toss.

I am by nature an impatient person. On the upside, I like to move quickly and get things going. The downside to this mindset however, is that things may get started that were not properly thought-through, not properly prepped or vetted.

When that happens, it's easy to wind up with a mess down the road. It's a delicate balance.

We need entrepreneurs and visionaries who see what's possible and push us forward—aggressively. We also need people who are gifted in execution, who understand how to fully and accurately count the cost of whatever new vision, mission, relationship, event, or service you are wanting to launch.

So today, before you move on to your next task, take just a moment to stop and reflect. What new thing are you currently building, launching, or releasing that would benefit from you taking some more time in thinking things through?

In short, where might you need to focus more on your toss in order to avoid dropping a ball down the road.

Keep juggling!

The Best Kind
of Glasses

get accused of a lot of things—most of it complimentary but certainly not every comment is positive.
Whether the comment is from my wife, a co-worker,
a client, or a friend, I try to objectively consider what
people have to say, consider their compliment or criticism, and learn from it.

One comment I hear a lot, and it's not without merit, is
that I tend to see things through "rose-colored glasses." I
admit it. I am an optimist, a glass-half-full kind of person.
I choose to see the best and believe the best in others and
in situations.

Yes, there is a danger in being naively optimistic. For
example, I would not be good in an HR position where
I had to screen resumes for a position and narrow down
the field of candidates to the top few. I tend to think every
candidate might be a potential superstar or a diamond in
the rough, even if their skill set doesn't match up well
with what the position requires. I am sometimes too quick
to jump into a new business relationship or partnership,

believing this is going to be "awesome" when others on my team tell me I am too trusting. They are sometimes right.

Yet we live in a culture that is becoming increasingly cynical, pessimistic, and where just five minutes of watching the evening news might lead you to believe along with Chicken Little that the proverbial sky is falling.

So while I think there is wisdom in being cautious, in taking a "trust but verify" approach, let me challenge you to make the choice to make your initial reaction, your first impression of a person, an opportunity or a circumstance, viewed from the perspective of: How could this work? What good could come from this? Then assume a best-case rather than worst-case result.

If you are not naturally wired to think this way, I appreciate that thinking positively is indeed a choice you have to make. But you can do it. Sometimes your intuitive gut-sense is that something's not right here, and in that case being cautious or critical is indeed the wiser approach to take. I trust you to know the difference between when a genuine internal red flag is waving versus you just naturally taking a more negative or guarded view.

But unless your internal warning system is sounding an alarm, try mentally exploring all the positive options that could result from whatever person or situation you are facing.

Go ahead, try on some rose-colored glasses this coming week. I dare you. You might just find that you enjoy the view.

Where Are You Settling?

As humans we have an unfortunate tendency to trade greatness for mediocrity, exchange dollars for dimes, and settle for average when amazing is just beyond our reach. Oh sure, there are the occasional stand-out leaders who have that knack for pressing through to greatness, who refuse to let their "life jars" get filled with assignments that others can do with equal aplomb and instead focus their attention, talent, and effort on achieving what they are called to do. They are driven by what stirs their passion and brings them maximum fulfillment and joy.

But what about the rest of us?

Why is it we find ourselves so easily distracted? Why do we naturally pursue the easier, but far less satisfying tasks first? When I go to the gym, I always do the elliptical machines first and save the dreaded treadmill runs till later in the week. Why do we procrastinate and put off the very thing that will bring the greatest reward?

I suspect there are many levels of answer to that question. The one we need to fight off the most is fear. Fear of failure. Fear of what others might think. Fear that the reality of our effort won't be as exciting as how we imagine it. It's easier just to stay too busy, too distracted, too overwhelmed, too tired, or even lazy to pursue our highest and best.

So how do we beat back the fear demon?

A couple thoughts that come to mind. The first is a passage from the Bible that says that "perfect love casts out fear" (1 John 4:18). The more our devotion to time with and focus on God grows, the more our confidence will grow. The more time I spend with the One who is perfect love, the more that love will rub off on me, and infuse my soul with the boldness that I need to conquer fear, to take the leap, to dream, and to risk as I was made to do. I need to look more into His eyes and less at my circumstances.

Secondly, make a spreadsheet. By nature, I am more of a "feeler" than a "thinker" so I don't always take the analytical approach to addressing a problem. But since perhaps you do, consider this. Make three columns. In one, list the benefits that would come to you if you pursued your dreams, your highest and best. In the next column, simply ask the "So What?" question. What's the worst that could happen if you pursue your highest and best and you fail? In the last column, list what will happen if you take the safe route and stick with status quo. Perhaps seeing the results of these three paths will provide the extra motivation you need to move from column three to column one!

You were born to do more than what you are doing right now.

Let's get busy!

Ten Things That Require Zero Talent

There are a lot of things in life that require special skill. Don't ask me to slam dunk a basketball. I might have all the passion and drive necessary to make that happen, but alas, my six-inch vertical leap just isn't going to get the job done. I can solder a broken wire—but I don't think you'd want me to do brain surgery on any of your relatives. Sure, we all could come up with a list of things we wish we were good at but just aren't. We are all uniquely gifted—just not equally gifted.

But instead of concentrating on what you cannot do, who you cannot be, here are ten things you can consistently do well regardless of your smarts, your physical prowess, your social skill, or your opportunity. These are ten things at which you can excel that require zero talent. Are you ready....

1. Being on time

2. Having a good work ethic

3. Doing your best

4. Having energy

5. Positive body language

6. Passion

7. Going the extra mile

8. Being prepared

9. Being teachable/coachable

10. Having a good attitude

I confess that my oldest son David sent me this list. His boss sent it to him. Today, take a few moments to consider the things that you are good at—or maybe they are things that are not "natural" to you, but still, doing them doesn't require a special talent or skill.

How about encouraging someone—it doesn't take any great skill to be nice, to say something positive, to notice when someone has made a change in their appearance. What if you decided not to gossip—choose not to get sucked into an unhealthy conversation? What if you assumed the best rather than the worst of someone else's motives? You see, throughout your day you have so many opportunities to make the world better—and it doesn't require you to be rich, famous, athletic, or gifted in any unique way. You are a world-changer. Start with your own world and work out from there!

Where Are You Playing "Peek-A-Boo"?

Ever play "Peek-a-Boo" with a baby? They close their eyes and assume because they can't see you, you're not there. Or you cover your eyes and say, "Wheeeeeeere's Joey?" You un-shield your eyes and shout, "Peek-a-Boo!" Joey laughs uncontrollably, and you smile.

Today I had someone come and wash my windows. It was way past time to get them cleaned. I called in Doug, a guy I'd used before and knew to be reliable and do good work. I didn't bother asking how much it was going to cost. I just knew it needed to be done. Throughout the day I found myself wondering, "I wonder what this is going to cost me?" But again, I never asked. That's not like me. I am typically a comparison shopper and tend to try and negotiate everything. But every once in a while, I find myself playing Peek-a-Boo, meaning that if I don't ask about the price, then the price isn't going to be bad.

Of course you can guess what happened. At the end of the day, Doug handed me his invoice. It was certainly reasonable and fair—but it was double what I was expecting, no hoping, it would be. Truth is, I didn't want to have to deal with the cost. I just wanted my windows done. So rather than be responsible and logical, I squeezed my eyes shut and played Peek-a-Boo.

Are there places in your life where you are playing Peek-a-Boo? For example, there's an unresolved tension with a co-worker. You know it's not going to go away, but you don't want to deal with it. So you play Peek-a-Boo, and avoid dealing with it. Is there a client you know is frustrated with you or someone you've known for years that you offended? Is there a debt you've put off paying down and instead keep rolling the debt forward month after month allowing the interest to continue to build? Don't play Peek-a-Boo with these matters. It never works out well.

I've heard it said that no sane person likes conflict. I'd like to think that's true. I suspect there are people who not only handle conflict well but in some twisted way it energizes them. So they stir it up because they find satisfaction in dealing with it. But for most of us, we are staunch conflict avoiders. We are masters at playing Peek-a-Boo.

So what's going on in your life right now that you need to face? What person or task or issue have you been avoiding, pretending that if you don't deal with it then it's not really there? May I respectfully encourage you to just deal with it. Face it. Stop playing Peek-a-Boo. I think you will find that the fruit of facing the things you would prefer to ignore will be well worth finding the courage to deal with them.

Don't Miss Your Moment of Opportunity

Despite all your best strategy and planning, sometimes the most important opportunities for your growth and success catch you by surprise. These moments are not predictable. For the most part, there's nothing you can do to force them to happen. What you can do, however, is be prepared to "seize the moment" when it comes.

Let me give you a recent for-instance. In 2021, Nicole Raviv was scheduled to sing the National Anthem at a Stanley Cup Playoff Game between the New York Islanders and the Boston Bruins NHL Hockey teams. She took the mic and began to sing. But a few seconds into the song, Nicole noticed how the fans who had packed New York's Nassau Coliseum (after a year of being cooped up due to Covid restrictions) were loudly and proudly singing along. Nicole had the presence of mind to drop her microphone so that the crowd's singing could be the focus of attention rather than her own. The result is that a simple singing of the National Anthem suddenly became national news and both internet and network news feeds all picked up the story. Nicole, while quite talented, would not be an A-list singer you've likely ever heard about ... but because of how she reacted in that moment, her nationwide exposure was through the roof.

Could she have planned for or predicted the crowd's reaction? Probably not. But her presence of mind in the moment catapulted her to new levels of recognition and, I suspect, opportunity.

Are there things in life, in relationship, and in business that you can plan for, prepare for, and train for? You bet. But to be ready for those serendipitous moments is more a matter of wisdom and character—and with perhaps a dash of good fortune thrown in for flavoring.

So what can you do to prepare yourself to "seize the moment?" I'm not sure there is any magic formula for this but here are some ideas to consider:

> **1. Get your heart right**—When you have a generous and caring heart, an outward focus on how you can help, support, and benefit others, that puts you in a better position to notice when a serendipitous moment arises. People who are overly focused on themselves tend to think small and narrow and will often miss a gift or blessing opportunity even when it's right in front of them.

> **2. Get your mind right**—Having an attitude of gratitude, a glass-half-full mindset, a positive way of thinking about life, helps you to see opportunity that others may overlook.

3. Cultivate excellence—When you are doing your job well, you are in a healthy position to react to an unexpected opportunity. People who are too busy putting out fires, dealing with drama in the office, or attending to an urgent matter or crisis don't have the time or emotional bandwidth to seize the moment of opportunity when it comes upon them. It's why lifeguards and police officers spend hours and hours of "readiness training," so that when a circumstance arises where they have to react to a life and death situation, something that can't be scheduled, flow-charted, or predicted, they will be ready.

So what can you do this week, what decisions can you make, that will help you be more prepared to seize your moment? May you have opportunity to both be blessed and extend a blessing to others. That's what makes life rich and rewarding.

Want to Get Ahead— Do What You Don't Want to Do

I recently read an e-newsletter from a friend I respect that was challenging me to pick up the phone and make calls. Arrrrrgh! I hate doing that. Don't get me wrong, I love connecting with people, and if you introduce me to someone to talk about publishing or marketing or parenting or living with purpose, anything about which I'm passionate, I will light up like a Christmas tree and share with enthusiasm about the work that I do. It has meaning to me and it helps people. Yet, if I am in a room full of prospective clients, I have to really push myself to reach out and make those contacts. Some people are great "hunters." They don't mind cold-calling and are good at it. Not me. Making prospecting calls is not something I enjoy doing. Consequently I resist it and look for anything else to do. And yet, making connections is the very thing I probably most need to do, at least at times.

Ever notice how easy it is to put off and avoid doing the things you don't want to do? Yet, oftentimes it's those things you want to avoid doing that you most need to do.

We all have things we don't like to do, things we tend to put off and avoid. Maybe it's having that hard conversation with a team member who is not pulling their weight, or making collection calls, or having to face a demanding customer whose business you value but their personality style, not so much. Whatever it is, make the commitment right now in your own heart and mind to get on it. What do stand-out performers do that others don't? Well, there are lots of answers to that question, but I know one of the answers is simply this ... they make themselves do the things they know they need to do. They let their vision for the future, their fire and passion for the end goal, help them push past their discomfort and procrastination.

What is it that you are avoiding? What is the task that you need to push past your procrastination and as the Nike Commercial would tell you, "Just do it!"?

Make the better choice today!

Where Are You Settling for Less?

One of the things I constantly wrestle with is the tension between striving for what's possible and at the same time being content with where I am. I never want to become too comfortable with the "status quo." Even when the current state is great, one of the worst things you can do is become complacent. You stop looking forward and looking for ways to improve, personally and professionally.

And yet, there is value in being "at peace" with who you are, where you are, and as you are. So how do you manage the tension between being happy with your current status and yet keep striving for more, to be better. If you've mastered this mystery, please email me and tell me how. I'm all ears (a rather weird image I suppose).

One thing I've observed in my own life is the tendency to slowly, over time, let some of the bigger dreams or visions die. Maybe not die, just become more distant and less pressing. It doesn't happen overnight—sort of like the old frog in the kettle analogy. Put the frog in the pot and turn up the heat slowly enough, the frog will be content to sit there and cook.

So today, as you read this, I want to challenge you, just as I am challenging myself, to take a step back and ask yourself where perhaps you have allowed the routine of life, maybe a series of small setbacks or disappointments, cause you to expect less, believe in less, and settle for less than what you should. Identify one life goal or perhaps a business goal that you once held on to that in recent years you've let go of. Ask yourself if that dream, that vision, was really supposed to die, or if perhaps you've just allowed the circumstances of life to cause you to settle for something less.

Identify one big thing—one dream—one BHAG (Big Hairy Audacious Goal) that if you don't do it, if you don't pursue it, it's not likely to happen.

May we both strive to pursue our highest and best, and not settle for less, together!

The Key to Fixing Big Problems—Think Small

This morning I read an email from a friend who is understandably concerned about the racial, political, social, and moral unrest and issues that are dividing us. He, like so many of us, has been watching various YouTube videos presenting some aspect of the problem but offering little or no solution. His email ended with, "So what are we to do?"

I got to thinking about that. The challenges we face as a nation, as a people, are complex. Take any of the recent protests we've seen on the news. It's a mixed bag ... there are genuine inequities that still exist. Some are deep and hurtful. Can these wounds be healed through public policy changes? Perhaps. But there are also cultural and economic issues that must be addressed as well. Can a child raised by a single mom succeed in life as well as a child raised in a two-parent home? Certainly. But the statistics show that it's harder. Can a child raised in poverty with limited educational options better themselves and create a more prosperous economic future for their children? Yes—but it's harder to do. And in the midst of it all there is raw emotion which sometimes leads to violence and irrational thinking that accomplishes nothing. And we all have some level of bias or prejudice, and people do use circumstances to promote their own political agendas. It's sad because it's hard to parse out and deal with one aspect of the situation without the interference of the other elements. We take sides and say that everything is either all wrong or everything is all justified.

Let me suggest that we will never solve anything, we will never move forward, as long as we hold to our sweeping generalizations. Instead, let's think small. Let's find one small piece of common ground that we can work on together. We can't solve the whole mess, but can we tackle one small piece and then move on to the next piece?

In tackling the coronavirus, do we really need to shut down everything, or quarantine everyone? Can we use a scalpel instead of a broad sword in tackling disease and injustice?

How about in your business? Do you need more leads? Are your expenses too high? What is one definitive area or aspect of your problem that you can commit to tackling this month and implementing change?

Sometimes the situation or the opportunity calls for a broad, bold move, for sweeping change. But most of the time ... making several, consistent, localized small changes is the path that will lead you out of your rut and into your promised land.

So today, take some time to step back and be intentional in making some small decisions. Start where you are. Use what you have. Do what you can.

Invest in What Matters Most

This past weekend, my wife Amy and I flew up to Atlanta to meet up with our oldest son David and his expectant wife Jeanna. From there, the four of us drove up into the mountains of North Carolina to see the fall colors and spend some time with Marshall and Sherrie, dear friends who have a mountain home that looks out over a lake and the breathtaking Blue Ridge Mountains. Living in Central Florida has lots of advantages but one of the things this Midwest-raised boy misses is the cooler and more colorful fall weather. It was nice to get away from the heat and flat topography of Florida.

It was a short trip and while the hiking and the scenery were grand, what really made the long weekend special was the time just sitting out on the deck, having great conversation, enjoying a glass of wine, savoring the relationships.

All sorts of external things bring us pleasure. We have favorite toys, favorite activities. But what I suspect most of us cherish most are those deeper relationships we have with family and friends—relationships that are forged over long periods of time. Deep relationships require that. They require an investment of time.

Whether you are polishing a stone or building a relationship, the process is just not something you can rush. Sadly, you and I have lives that are filled with "rushing." I seldom get everything on my daily to-do list checked off. There is always more to do than I can accomplish. There is always the mounting pressure to get in one more thing, accomplish one more task, call one more client, fit in one more meeting or event. I confess I am guilty of valuing my day, even my vacations, by how many things I got done, how many things on my list I got checked off. Even my weekends are rated by how many projects or chores I got done.

But relationships, at least the really good ones, take time. They happen over a lifetime of being present, showing up, putting yourself out there. I love the relationship I have with each of my sons, and now my daughters-in-law. I am spending time now going to my grandkids' soccer games and dance recitals and just having pillow fights in the family room. Each on their own is not a big deal and if I wasn't there, it wouldn't be a big deal. But all the time we spend with someone else adds up and becomes the seasoning that makes for a profoundly satisfying relationship.

So as you move through the hectic seasons of life, as your normal routines get interrupted with all sorts of extra events and obligations, remember to sow into the relationships that matter to you the most. It's a slow process. Sometimes it takes conscious effort. But you are investing in something special, even sacred, that has the potential to enrich your life immeasurably.

Want Your Business to Grow? Change Your Perspective

The other day I was talking with a friend of mine—a truly gifted musician and writer. Both his music and his writing touch people deeply because there is a vulnerability, an honesty, to his work that people appreciate. My friend freely shares his own struggles, his own questioning and insecurities and in the process gives his audience permission to feel, to dream and to be OK with their own flaws. But when I went to his website, all I saw was product offerings. Buy this book. Check out this new album. He was guilty of a cardinal marketing sin. His marketing was communicating to his audience from his perspective, not theirs. He was showing and telling what he wanted to share, not what they wanted to see.

I see this all the time. An incredible charity tells me what they are doing instead of how I can make a difference in someone's life. A financial planner tells me about his track record in picking great stocks instead of how wonderful I would feel knowing my financial future was secured. A personal trainer demonstrates his unique training techniques, not how I can regain the washboard abs of my twenties.

My point is simply this—take time to evaluate your public presentation, your website, your flyers, your YouTube videos, your Facebook ads, your eblasts. Are you communicating from the perspective of what you want to share or what your audience wants to feel, to learn, to know, or to experience? Perspective changes everything.

May you "see" things more clearly and gain a fresh perspective that incites your business to grow.

Are You Easily Offended?

The political and cultural climate in our country has gotten awfully testy, don't you think? Seems to me everyone is looking for an excuse to be offended. We all have thin skin and thick hearts. I think it should be the other way around. We ought to have a thicker skin and a more tender heart.

It's almost as if every special interest group is looking to pick a fight with the world. Why is that? How is this helping us get along, live together, and make progress towards solving problems that all of us would agree need fixing?

Throughout my professional career I've rubbed up against some pretty crusty people—people who are quick to find fault, criticize, offer unsolicited advice, and provide an opinion that seems more like a put-down than a sincere attempt to make me better. Sound familiar? When that happens, how do you handle it? Are you quick to slip into self-doubt, to find yourself thinking, "Yeah, they're right, I'm really not cut out for this"?

Instead of assuming the worst, how about taking a different path. Don't be so quick in your immediate mental dialog to put yourself down, second-guess your effort or motives. Assume you are doing an amazing job and are an amazing person. Then, from that initial assumption of greatness, go ahead and consider the criticism. See if indeed there is a better way, something you can learn from the negative comment. Even if your mental assessment reveals that yes, you could have done or handled that situation better, don't let that translate into believing you are not a noble, valued, prized, and beloved person—someone who is exactly who they should be and where they should be in that moment.

Let's work at not being so quick to get our emotional noses out of joint, get huffy, defensive, and upset. Be like the proverbial duck and let the negativity, like water, roll right off your back. Yes, still be teachable and self-aware enough to note where you can improve but even in that, rejoice in the knowledge that you are just getting better!

Today, may you get more and more excited about who you are and what you can accomplish!

Now go make a positive difference in the world.

The Building Blocks of Personal and Corporate Growth

Just this morning I was on the phone with a client. We had started a ghostwriting project with them and the first draft just didn't turn out the way either of us hoped. Capturing someone's story in the right way, with the right tone and "voice" is not an exact science. So we both agreed to start over. Things like this happen all the time. We all face circumstances that knock us back, throw us for a loop. When that happens what do you do? You can choose to make excuses, focusing on who is to blame. You can choose to focus on the quickest way to get back on track—like when your GPS tells you that you just missed the exit. It immediately recalculates to help you find the quickest way to get back on course. You can choose to lament over the consequences of the error, how much time you lost, or added expense you incurred.

Let me suggest a fourth perspective—how about focusing on what you learned from the mistake and how you can shore up your systems, change your process, or build in added safeguards to ensure that this type of mistake doesn't happen again. This is how we get better. The wise leader pays attention to learning from mistakes. Many publishing agreements are ten to fifteen pages long. Why, because every time the publisher gets burned, they add another clause to their contracts to make sure that situation can't happen again.

My point is, the way we grow both personally and corporately is often times through our mistakes.

If you've ever taken the DISC personality test, you know the "D" represents the dominant type of personality, the leader willing to take risks, to break the status quo, to push the boundaries in order to move ahead. They are also the first to look for ways to make a system or a circumstance better when something goes wrong. This focus on learning from our mistakes is what helps us grow and get better.

Of course it's always good to surround these "D-leaders" with others who can have empathy for those impacted by the error, and those who can analyze the situation best, those who can pick up the broken pieces, whether they are literal pieces or emotional pieces, and those who can help us laugh through the pain.

Since despite our best efforts we can't avoid making mistakes or bumping into circumstances that throw us off course, let's make a point to always ask ourselves, "What can we learn from this? How can we grow from this and how can we get better and be better?"

May every step you take this week move you forward and upward!

The Transitions We Celebrate

This week I celebrated a new life coming into the world. My son and daughter-in-law brought a precious little five-pound peanut into the world, Breelan Cady Welday. What a joy. She just left a very comfortable thirty-six week existence to be birthed into a new world of lights, sounds, hugs, oooohs and ahhhhhs combined with other things new to her such as feeding, diapers, burping, hiccups, and an uncomfortable amount of probing by well-meaning nurses. I'm sure the transition for baby Breelan was abrupt and unsettling ... she doesn't yet know all the wonders that await her.

This same week a beloved figure, Dr. Billy Graham, made his own transition from this life to a new life that I'm sure will be for him even more wondrous than the one Breelan will now experience.

I celebrate them both.

Truth is, we all face a series of transitions—from being potty-trained, to having a driver's license, to losing a parent, or spouse or child, to seeing kids off to college, to losing a job or being promoted to a new job. How do we handle them? I say, pop the champagne—let's celebrate! Why? Because transitions, both the fun ones and the hard and horrible ones, happen to all of us. We can't avoid them. But we can learn from them and grow through them. I often say, "Let your refining moments become your defining moments."

They say attitude is everything. That's probably not quite true but close enough. Choose to embrace your transitions. Look for ways to benefit from them and be a benefit to others going through their own transitions. Celebrate knowing that these transitions have to potential to make you better.

Sometimes you have to make the determined choice to make that happen. But isn't that better than the alternative? There's nothing noble about becoming a victim even though it might feel comforting for a short while. Let's celebrate life, both the brand-new ones (like my granddaughter), the ninety-nine-year-old kind (like Billy Graham), and all the important, sometimes life-altering transitions that happen in between.

Your Response Makes All the Difference

I spent time recently with a dear friend who is struggling with cancer ... she's been in this fight for seven years. Whenever we are confronted with real human trauma, it reminds us just how fragile life is. We get so easily wrapped around the axle over things that really don't matter.

Just this morning I was fussing (mostly to myself), about needing to install a new dishwasher, paint the upstairs bathroom, and fix a shelf in the kitchen that I just don't have time to get to ... first world problems. These are things that in the grand scheme of things don't matter. Why let these "little things" rob us of our joy or cause us to lose focus on doing things that really matter in life?

Right now you are facing some challenges. I know that because everybody has things in life that they need to tackle. We all got issues! The question though is not how serious or numerous are your issues but how will you respond to them.

We can't choose our circumstances. We can only choose our response.

So today, my encouragement to you is to lift up your head, smile, be grateful for who you are and what you have and choose to respond well to whatever life throws at you. Your attitude affects your outlook.

Don't Discount the Impact You Have

Most people are not all that impressed with themselves. It's understandable. We are all-too-aware of our shortcomings and flaws. We all know people who are more talented, gifted, fortunate, or favored than we are. So while we can put on a good mask and work to convey confidence, inside we know where we have fallen short of our potential and in some cases downright messed up.

Yet despite your failures and flaws, you have an amazing potential to inspire, bless, lift up, defend, embolden, and encourage others. You probably do it more often than you know. Each of us has an incredible opportunity every day to breathe hope, vision, confidence, and courage into others. Don't discount the impact you are having on others.

In fact, take a moment even as you finish reading this to pause and consider, who are the people in your life that take strength and encouragement from you? They are there. I have an author friend, David Buehring, who once told me, "Pay attention to those in whose ears your voice is loud." Who are you influencing? Who are the people paying attention to you and how you respond in different situations?

Is it your children? Your neighbors? Your spouse? Your co-workers? How about the random people you run into throughout your week—the server in a restaurant, the checkout girl at the grocery store, the person you sit next to on an airplane. Each of these are people whose lives can be enriched by YOU. You don't have to be a philanthropist, pastor, or pontificator of "deep truths." You just have to be a person who pays attention to the opportunities all around you. You just have to be willing to be generous with your kindness, your encouragement, your helpfulness, your wisdom, and experience.

I suspect, or at least I hope, that one day the eternal curtain will be pulled back and you will have the chance to see just how much good, how much positive influence, you have had on the lives of so many people. You don't have to be rich, noble, or famous—just be you and be available.

So this week, be intentional on focusing less on your failures and more on the opportunities that abound for you to be a person of positive influence and impact. It will make your day!

Baggy Pants

Recently I was giving a presentation to a group of up-and-coming leaders. It was a casual gig and so I was dressed appropriately (or so I thought) in my jeans and an untucked shirt. Problem is, my jeans were so baggy that you could probably hide the Idaho potato truck in there and nobody would notice. My wife tried to warn me before I headed out, but I was late and didn't heed her call to change pants. Near the end of the presentation, the host who introduced me made fun of those pants. The crowd laughed. I laughed. But I got the message.

In both life and business you likely have some things you are carrying that frankly need to go. Goodwill might not even want them. I'm not talking about out-of-date clothes (though if the proverbial shoe fits...), I'm talking about habits, attitudes, processes—things that you've been doing the same way for too long. Things that when you were younger or in a less strategic position in your company didn't matter—but now they do. Maybe you joke a little too inappropriately. Maybe you're always a few minutes late. Maybe your website hasn't been updated in four years (which these days is a long time).

My point is, we are all carrying some "baggy pants" that need to go. Why haven't they gone already? Probably because you haven't cared and assume that since you don't care, nobody else does either. News flash. People notice. You want to be a person of influence? You probably already are. So live your life and run your business as if others are watching. Be a standard bearer for excellence. Just because something worked for you in the past, doesn't mean it's still working. Just because something went unnoticed or was tolerated in the past doesn't mean that it's OK to keep doing it. Frankly, the higher up the ladder of influence you want to climb, the more refined your life needs to be. The pot metal that forms the housing of my lawn mower is not nearly as refined and high-grade of steel as the housing of a Boeing 737 jet engine. The stresses on that engine housing and the consequences if it fails are much greater than for my lawn mower. So it is with you. The more influence you have (or want to have), the more people who are watching, the more customers that you serve, the less you can afford to tolerate a bad habit, out-of-date process, or ineffective employee.

Are there some baggy pants in your closet that need to go?

Let's soar high and far this year and make a positive difference in the lives of others!

Consistency Counts

When it comes to building a company, a fellow-ship, a community, or a family, knowing the right thing to do is important. Determining your values, the things that you stand for, the priorities you place on people, on excellence, on innovation, etc., these are all critical aspects of creating something that lasts. However, these things alone won't get you where you want to be.

In establishing these things, there is another key factor you must consider, and that's your ability to consistently execute. It's one thing to decide on your "core values" as a company or what will be the rules of the house when it comes to doing chores. It's quite another to be able to consistently execute those things over long periods of time.

When I was growing up, my bed always had to be made and made properly—not just whenever my mom and dad thought about it, but every day, rain or shine. That was the house rule. Now if I had been the perfect child and always did this without fail, enforcing this house rule would have been easy. But it took an incredible amount of energy and attention from my dad. After a hard day at the office, the last thing I'm sure he wanted to do was inspect my room and then have to take the time and energy to call me back in from whatever I was doing to correct the bed-making if upon his inspection it wasn't done right.

It's the same in business. It's easy to say you will answer every email or customer complaint within twenty-four hours. But do you have the systems in place to monitor that this is what's really happening? Do you have the will to follow-up and enforce your rules consistently? It takes a lot of effort and commitment. But this is how families and companies, organizations and individuals build a brand, build a reputation that people respect and remember. It's not just how clever or creative their policies and practices are. It's how consistently those policies and practices are being implemented. Bottom line: execution is everything.

So as you set your goals and objectives over the next months, make sure you not only come up with the right things to target. Make sure you have the systems and the will to enforce these things consistently. Consistency counts!

Your Words Matter

You've heard it said that the pen is mightier than the sword. That saying (I had to look it up), came from British author Edward Bulwer-Lytton, who in 1839 penned that phrase in a play to convey that in his view, written words were more effective than violence in communicating a point.

But what about the words we say....

I believe there is something mystically powerful about spoken words. Words have the power to pierce flesh and blood and both wound and inspire the human soul. Mental health counselors and psychologists make a lot of money and spend hours of time undoing the damage that spoken words have done.

How many precious sons and daughters marvelously made in the image of God have thought less of themselves or settled for an incomplete or inaccurate assessment of their worth because they were told, perhaps over and over, that they were not good enough, smart enough, pretty enough, talented enough.

Maybe the damage was done not by written or spoken words but by "mind words," the thoughts we tell ourselves. Are there unhealthy thoughts that you secretly harbor? Just because the words you hear may be negative doesn't mean they are harmful. If I'm walking around with my fly down, I appreciate someone inconspicuously pointing that out. If I have a bad habit of chewing food with my mouth open or dominating conversations, I will be wise to listen to corrective counsel, even if it's hard to hear. However, there is a difference between corrective counsel that is based on truth and negative words based on a lie. It's the lies we hear in our head, that we sometimes tell ourselves, that can be so destructive. How do you conquer those lies? One way is to override the lies in your head by speaking words of truth out loud. Here's where we can help each other.

If you have a co-worker or a friend you know is beating themselves up internally in an unhealthy way, you can help by speaking positive truth to them. Your spoken words alone may not be the solution, but they can help. Truth is, we choose to believe what we want. I can tell a friend that they are amazingly gifted and a beautiful person all day long. But I can't keep that friend from choosing to embrace an internal lie that they are nothing but a screw-up.

My challenge to you today, is not to try and save the world through your words ... but to just be intentional in choosing to speak light and love, truth and value to yourself and to others every chance you get. Words matter.

Are you a "Lawn Mower Leader?" I heard a new term the other day: "Lawn mower parents." The term is used to define a mom or dad who "mows down every obstacle" facing their child so they don't have to struggle with the consequences that obstacle presents.

It sounds noble enough. I mean, what parent doesn't want to help their child avoid conflict and pain? The problem is that as humans we were made to struggle. It's how we grow. Take away our pain, our difficulty, and we become fragile and unable to cope well when adversity (which is unavoidable) ultimately comes.

Did you know that the average millionaire goes bankrupt 3.5 times? We all get knocked down in life. The key is how quickly we get back up.

So don't fear adversity or failure. These are often the essential ingredients to success. Instead, develop resiliency, a mindset, a belief system that allows you to handle challenges and difficult circumstances well. If you do, you will not only embrace a key character trait necessary for your own success, you will be in a better position to be there for the person next to you when they fall.

What's the "Good" Behind the Work You Do?

We all want to do good work. We want to know that what we are investing a major portion of our lives into matters, that what we do makes a difference. So take a moment to consider just what is the "good" behind the good work that you do.

Consider this. At first blush I might say, "At HigherLife, I work to publish and market books." A true statement. But is that really the good work that I am doing? Let's press in further. What if I say, "I don't just publish books. I help authors share stories—stories of impact, stories that make the world a better place." That's better.

But I submit that there is deeper, more profound good work that we do. When we published Alisa Jordheim's book *Made in the USA, The Sex Trafficking of America's Children*, we helped her awaken people to the horrific reality of the sex trafficking underworld. We are playing a part in helping a twelve-year-old girl in Houston, Texas or a nine-year-old boy in Omaha, Nebraska be set free from their captors and get the counseling they need to have at least the shot of living a full and productive life—a life that can positively impact their future children, grandchildren, and generations to come.

When we published Donald Clinebell's book *The Service Driven Leader*, we helped him inspire thousands of men and women to devote more of their time and talent to worthy service projects. These projects can result in a middle school child in Columbus, Ohio who might have joined a gang just to feel a sense of belonging, to instead find a mentor that gives him the courage and the hope to stay in school. We are providing water to hundreds of villagers in a small village outside of Rwanda who will now have drinking water and be able to attend a single-room school house.

Maybe you are a plumber—do you just repair leaks or do you help a single mom be able to stay in her home and provide lunches for her fourth grade child as he heads off to school? Maybe you do analytics for an insurance company—do you just run spreadsheets or do you make it possible to provide a safety net for hundreds of thousands of people? In fact, seventeen of those people would be homeless due to a fire or flood that ravaged their street but because of their insurance, they can stay in a hotel for three months until the damage has been repaired.

My point is that what you do is more impactful, more important, more significant than you probably realize.

So take some time this week to consider the "good work" that you are doing. Make it your mission this week to help others to see the good and meaningful impact that they are having in the world because of what they do and how they show up.

Are You Producing Music or Noise?

I have a couple dear friends who are really good for me. They both remind me that I need to build into my life room to breathe, to think, to dream, to process, and to pray. The first is Chris Maxwell. Chris and I have known each other for years. Chris is a gifted writer, speaker, and editor who's written a series of books themed around the title, *Pause*. His message is just what you'd expect—that we need to take time in our lives to pause, in order to optimize our effectiveness and impact. I need to hear that—often!

The second friend is Dr. Jon Davis, a pastor, speaker, and musician who until recently served as executive director of Canterbury Retreat and Conference Center. Jon takes regular time away for personal retreat, to gain new direction and insight, to listen to God as well as his own heart. Jon challenges me to do the same.

Both of these men understand that our lives get very busy, very fast. We often confuse effort with impact and busyness with productivity. Neither is true. How often have you come home from a hard day's work and your spouse asks an innocent question: "So what did you do today?" Simple enough, right? Yet, when you reflect back, you realize you created a lot of motion, a lot of effort; **you made noise throughout your day, but you didn't necessarily make music.** There's a difference. Both produce sound. But one has direction, a rhythm, and melody, harmony and structure that is pleasing. It creates energy and emotion. It can stimulate or soothe. By contrast, noise is just irritating. It unnerves and tires you.

How can you do a better job making music throughout your day instead of just noise? Here are two suggestions. First take time in your week to think, to dream, to reflect, to listen, to strategize, and to plan. Secondly make a plan and stick to it. Build in space for the unforeseen and unexpected. But decide what are the things you have to get done, then go do those first.

Now let's you and I make some great music this week!

You Are a Person of Influence

Yesterday I had lunch with a new friend, Alexandria. We are co-teaching a marketing seminar together so I wanted to get to know her better. As I often do, I opened our conversation with a simple question, "So, tell me your story." Alex began to share about her upbringing, how her father had such an incredible influence on her life. Shortly after she was born, her parents split up. When Alex was five, she went to live with her dad. A single father taking on the responsibility to raise a young child is a sacrificial act of love. I'm sure it was not easy. Today, as a young woman, Alex has an entrepreneurial spirit, a confidence in herself and an enthusiasm about life that's infectious. It's also rare. She is quick to credit her dad for this. The way he raised her, loved her, and poured into her life as she grew up is now being reflected in Alex's bright and winsome personality and positive outlook on life.

What I want to challenge you to stop and consider is this: who are the people in your life where you have the unseen power of influence to build up and encourage?

One of our clients, David Buehring, says, "Pay attention to those in whose ears your voice is big." I like that. You have so much opportunity to make someone's day, to help someone grow, to shape someone's outlook on life. Don't get so busy, so caught up in your own world that you miss out on being the person of influence you were meant to be.

Freefall, the Secret to Mastering Your Fears

We all face fear. In many ways, fear is one of the most powerful influencers in your life. There's a healthy kind of fear, like the kind that causes you to duck when you hear a loud bang, or you're on the golf course and someone shouts, "FORE!" Our built-in inclination for survival has given us the gift of fear to help us stay alive and avoid calamity.

But there is a far more insidious and pervasive kind of fear that plagues us all. It shows up in lots of ways—fear of failure, fear of rejection, fear of what others will think, fear of the unknown, fear of change, fear of loss—and yet each of us who lives in this world lives with all these things. They are unavoidable. So how do you conquer your fear, or at least not let it keep you from experiencing your highest and best potential? I recently read a chapter from a book written by a friend of mine, Dave Brisbin. The book is titled *Daring to Think Again* and the chapter is aptly titled, "Freefall." In this particular chapter Dave describes in detail the day he went skydiving for the first time. Talk about facing your fears! In the book Dave shares that you can read about something and listen to the tales of others who've experienced it. You can watch videos, learn all the facts, know all about a thing or an experience. But you never really know it until you do it. So it is with skydiving. So it is with just about anything in life.

Dave's a good writer so his words created images in my mind. I could picture myself with him standing in the middle of this gaping hole in the side of this metal tube flying at 12,500 feet above the ground, wind whipping across my face, his fingers white as they tightly gripped the opposing edges of that opening. Right up to that moment, Dave still had a choice. He could go forward or back out. He had similar choices throughout the day, as he drove up to the airfield, as he was getting instruction, as he was signing the legal waivers, as he stepped into that metal tube with wings. And as long as he had choices, he felt fear. Which would he choose? What would be the consequences of his choices?

What struck me most in this chapter was this statement: **"As soon as I let go and left all my choices behind, I wasn't afraid anymore."** In an instant, Dave went from fear to exhilaration and being totally in the moment.

As long as we have something to cling to, as long as we have a choice, a decision to make, one that could lead to exhilaration and joy but could also result in calamity, shame, failure, or worse, we will carry fear. Life, like sky-diving, is a journey, an adventure, and along the path we have so many decisions to make. So many choices. With those decisions comes fear. So how do you live your life with less fear? Move forward. Let go. Stop clinging to the edge of the doorway. Trust. Truth is, your whole life is a freefall anyway. The safety of that airplane is an illusion. You can do this!

What Do You Celebrate?

I recently read an e-newsletter that made the comment that the things that we celebrate are the substance of our story. I'm paraphrasing here. But as you know, I am passionate about helping people discover their authentic story and helping them find creative ways to share that story as a means to positively impact the lives of others. That's really what HigherLife is all about—it's not just about publishing a book or building a website. It's about sharing our story with others. We do this not to draw attention to ourselves but because we know that there is something in our own story, our own journey, that can be a source of inspiration and encouragement to others.

Think about the things that you celebrate in life ... not just the personal achievements but the milestones, the values, the significant events that define who you are and how you want to be remembered.

Consider making a list of your top ten things to celebrate. You might want to break your list into categories: for example, things that you will still be celebrating ten years from now, versus things that are worth celebrating now but ten months, ten weeks or even ten days from now, not so much.

As you make your list what stands out to you? Is there a common theme behind the life stories that you celebrate? As you see the pattern you may be getting closer to identifying your life's purpose and call.

Nothing makes your life more meaningful than living it according to your core purpose, your divine call. I believe that every person was uniquely and divinely created with design and intention. It makes sense, doesn't it? After all, everything that is made, is made for a purpose. A stapler, a pen, a phone, a medicine—everything. So if we create things on purpose and for a purpose, doesn't it make sense that you too are created with intentionality and purpose? Don't live your life merely reacting to circumstances. Discover your purpose and live your life aligned around that purpose. Taking note of the things you celebrate may be an important step in your pursuit of personal discovery.

Which Brain Are You Using?

The other day I did a radio interview for a business show. I was on with another gentleman who was talking about how to market products appealing to our three brains—Three, huh? There are times my wife might question whether I have even one functioning brain, much less three. But alas, neuroscientists affirm that inside our heads we actually have three brains—OK, to be fair, we have one brain with three distinct parts.

It just sounds better to say we have three brains. Here they are:

1. Your Lizard Brain or Gut Brain—technically the medulla or brainstem—this is the smallest part of your brain connected to your spinal cord, your doing brain where autonomic functions such as breathing and blinking occur. Your basest instincts for survival and mating occur here.

2. Your Wolf Brain or Heart Brain—technically the limbic system or cerebellum—this is your feeling brain, where you experience emotion and memories.

3. Your Human Brain or Head Brain—technically the cerebrum—this is the largest part of your brain and where you do most of your thinking, processing, and logic.

So the answer to my question, which part of the brain are you using, is simple—all of them—all the time!

The challenge for us when trying to communicate is to target our communication to the right part of the brain. For example, in any form or marketing you want to follow this simple process:

1. Grab attention

2. Create desire

3. Build trust

4. Generate action

So ask yourself, what part of the brain do you want to target when grabbing attention? I suppose that depends on what you are selling. In general though the lizard brain or gut brain is where you want to focus.

In terms of creating desire and hunger for what you are offering, well, emotion wins hands down. Target the limbic system or wolf/heart brain. Simon Sinek in his book *Start with Why* did a masterful job of presenting the case for appealing to this part of our brains when communicating.

When it comes to building trust, earning respect, that's more of a human/head brain function. Trust has to be earned.

Life is hard. We get knocked down a lot, so it's no wonder many of us sometimes struggle with issues of self-worth. So take a moment to ponder and appreciate just how wonderfully complex and brilliantly made you are. An ancient king once penned that as humans we are "fearfully and wonderfully made." I agree. I'm amazed that any doctor or scientist could not believe in God. The wonder of how we are intricately woven together is an amazing thing.

So this week, make a point to pay attention to, appreciate, and communicate well with your other three-brained mammals called humans!

May you see yourself as the truly amazing creation that you are.

Stale Bread Is for the Birds

As I write this I'm at the beach enjoying some family time with kids and grandkids. One of the simple pleasures is watching little kids feed the seagulls pieces of leftover bread. The thing is, stale bread isn't good for too much other than feeding the birds. Food, much like business, needs to stay fresh.

I recently was talking to a colleague of mine who told me about a former company we both did work for. Their business, which at one time was thriving, recently closed up shop with their assets being sold off for pennies on the dollar. In the wake of this closure vendors were left unpaid and workers unemployed. Very sad.

What happened? Here's my take. The owners who had built up the business were not willing to stay current with market trends. They failed to take appropriate risk. They didn't innovate. Their product line became stale. As a result, they gradually lost market share and eventually got so overwhelmed with debt that they couldn't recover.

Business and life operate similarly. You get too comfortable with what you have to where you lose your willingness to dream, to risk, to innovate, and what happens? Over time, you lose. It happens in sports all the time. One team gets a comfortable lead and so they stop playing offense. They start playing just defense, working to hold on to their lead. As a result, the other team comes from behind, builds momentum, and ultimately wins the game.

Growth always involves looking ahead, taking risk, dreaming and looking over the horizon to where you're going. Yes, occasionally glance in your rear-view mirror. Celebrate your accomplishments. Learn from the past. But keep your eyes, mind, and heart looking forward to what lies ahead. Is it scary sometimes? Yes. Is there the possibility of making a mistake, of failure? Certainly. So surround yourself with people smarter than you. Talk to people who have been where you are headed. Be willing to be the least knowledgeable or successful person in your group. It will keep you both humble and hungry for more. Both are good. Oh, and enjoy the ride. The unexpected and the unknown are like seasoning that spices up a meal to make it memorable.

Look Who Believes in You

Life can be hard. Despite our "game face," inside we all wrestle with some degree of self-doubt.

One of the greatest gifts you can receive is having someone in your life who believes in you—and they're not silent about it. They tell you. A person who notices a particular talent, skill, ability, or characteristic that you possess and reminds you of it often is truly someone special. Perhaps you were blessed to have a parent or grandparent early on in life who took note of you and was faithful to pour their faith, encouragement, and positive affirmation into you. Be grateful for that. Even now, as you are actively pursuing your dreams, working hard, and tending to others, do you have someone in your life who consistently reminds you of your own greatness, of your own unique talents and abilities? That's a gift to truly treasure.

So let me ask you, who is in your life, who comes to mind where you can be the gift? Who do you know that has a fantastic smile, a knack for numbers, an incredible voice, a way with words? It doesn't matter what the personality trait or skill set is, what matters is that you celebrate it. You tell them.

I have a good friend named Marshall who often tells me that he thinks I am one of the most creative people he's ever met. My first reaction is usually something like, "Well then you need to get out and meet more people!" But inside, my heart is affirmed by his words of encouragement. They inspire me to be more creative, to exercise the gift or ability God has given me.

So my encouragement to you is to be grateful for the people who believe in you and be intentional in looking for that person to whom you can be that gift.

May you be an amazing gift to the world by how you live today!

How Not to "Win" an Argument

The biggest communication problem we have is that we do not listen to understand. We listen to reply.

I wrote down this phrase in my notes because I thought it was powerful and something that I need to remind myself regularly. I only wish I knew where I heard this so I could give proper credit. But regardless of who said it first, the statement, I believe, is nonetheless true.

How many times have you caught yourself thinking of the answer you intend to give even before the other person pauses to take a breath? I know I'm guilty. How often have I sat quietly listening to someone else share, mainly because I count on them giving me the same courtesy when it's my turn. Sadly, we are often not really that interested in what someone is saying to us. But we sure hope that what we say has the desired impact and dazzles the other party.

Sigh ... If most people think this way, I suspect not much will ever get done.

There have been books written and seminars taught (and probably a lot of money made) on effective communication. I doubt I will share anything here that hasn't been said a thousand times before and probably in more compelling ways.

So let me offer this simple reminder. Whatever you want to accomplish, whatever goals you desire to achieve, whether in business, finances, ministry, or relationships, you likely will not achieve these goals alone. You need other people—you need to work with other people ... and people out there also need you. And anytime we are forced to work together, that requires communication.

When communication is a contest where you "win" by getting someone to agree, listen to you more, or succumb to your way of thinking, I submit you've already lost.

My wife and I sometimes meet with young couples contemplating marriage to do pre-marital counseling. I let both sides know that their goal in communication is not for one side to win but that the marriage wins. Both sides working and communicating together so that the relationship thrives. That is a higher, more noble objective than for either side to get their way or win over their partner to their way of thinking.

So the next meeting or intense conversation you have, go into that conversation with the goal not that you will "convince" the other person. Instead, listen to genuinely HEAR the other person. You should both be clear in the objective of working together to accomplish or achieve whatever sparked the need for the conversation. When you do that—then a communication "win" is indeed possible.

When Taking Longer and Doing It Wrong Is Right

Have you ever tried to teach a young child a new skill? It can be painstaking. As a kid, it was my job not just to cut the grass but "manicure the lawn." That meant cutting the grass, edging the garden and sidewalks, and pulling weeds. Early on in my "career" as a home-grown landscape architect, my father spent countless hours making me go back and redo spots that I missed, going back over places in the grass where I didn't properly let the lawnmower wheels overlap the rows so as to not leave fine strips of uncut lawn.

Even fun projects you do with your kids like making cookies take twice as long and make double the mess than if you just did it yourself. And yet you gladly take the extra time and put up with the additional mess. Why?

The answer is it's an investment in your child's growth and development. You see, getting better at virtually anything can be messy. But the wise parent, as well as the gifted manager or leader, understands that sometimes it's better to allow something to be done wrong in order for your child, your student, your up-and-coming manager, to learn from their mistakes. It's how we grow. It's how we mature and get better. Sometimes the most expedient, the most efficient path to completion, is not the best.

My friend Chris Maxwell was sharing with me how, when the bridge in north Atlanta collapsed due to a fire, people needing to get to the airport had to discover alternate routes. The most efficient and direct path to their destination (in a city already infamous for its traffic congestion) was no longer available. Having to explore new routes you make new discoveries, a new restaurant to try, some beautiful scenery you've never seen before, a fun shop to explore. Life can be like that. Sometimes the longer, less efficient path provides windows to new discoveries, new ideas, new ways to approach a problem.

So this week, whether you are investing in another person, or simply taking time to invest in your own soul, your own way of thinking about a situation, consider the longer, slower, messier approach. You might just make someone else better for it ... or become the better person yourself.

Turn Off Your Edger

There's no denying that our world has become more hectic, more "noisy." We keep multiple to-do lists, constantly overbook and take on too many projects. And let's be honest, we've become comfortable with that. With all that activity, certainly lots gets done. But some things suffer in the process. We don't give ourselves adequate time to process, to think, to dream, to imagine. And our relationships sometimes suffer as well. We see the people we need to see but we don't truly let people in. We become busier on the outside, yet more isolated on the inside.

What's the solution? Well besides the obvious answer, which is to simplify your schedule a bit, let me suggest this: in your interactions with people, take time to pause, to take a breath, and actually listen to what the other person is saying. I don't mean just listen with your ears, but listen with your mind and heart.

When I was a kid growing up, weekends were usually filled with yardwork. My dad, my brother, and sister, we all had assignments. I don't remember exactly where the saying initiated but I remember my mom telling my dad to

"Turn off your edger," which was a euphemism to remind him to stop his yard work (which was often edging the driveway and sidewalks) long enough to listen to what my mom or one of the kids were trying to ask him. Turn off your edger meant, "Focus, Danielson, focus!" Don't half listen while still trying to get one more thing checked off your weekend to-do list.

So in the midst of your hectic and noisy life, make sure you are intentional about listening, not just to what is being said, but with close attention to the person saying it. Who knows, some of your greatest insights, your next "Ah-Ha!" moment might come from being open and vulnerable enough to really listen.

This kind of "active listening" actually takes a bit of work, some getting used to. But try it even today, in your next work conversation, instead of thinking about your response while the other person is still talking, try doing just one thing, really listening. Turn off your mental edger and listen. You might be pleasantly surprised at the insights that come to you as a result.

What Are You Afraid Of?

Recently I met with an incredibly successful business man. He climbed the corporate ladder and achieved success most of us only dream about. From stock boy to vice president this guy consistently exceeded expectations and rose to the top. Everything looked great on the outside.

Problem was that what was motivating him to achieve was fear. Fear of failure, fear of not being good enough, fear of not being accepted. Fear of what others might think. As a result, despite all the fame and fortune this guy spent decades in therapy. Only recently has he emerged from the shadows of all that internal angst to find peace with himself.

Fear can sometimes be a great motivator but it's best used in short bursts. You know the fight or flight syndrome. You see a bear in your yard (which actually happened to us just recently) and you high-tail it inside fast. But fear is not a good long-term motivator. A friend called me to ask for some advice in deciding between two job offers he was wrestling with. My comment—"Don't let fear be the determining factor in your decision. Both jobs have exciting opportunity but both come with a certain amount of risk. Make your decision based on the upside potential, the sense of calling and the opportunity to make a difference."

We all deal with fear. Fear has its place. But too often we let fear drive us. We were meant for something greater.

The Power of Simplicity

Most of us have too much on our plates—too many things on our to-do lists. On top of that, we fill in the cracks of our already jam-packed schedules by scrolling through Facebook posts or Twitter feeds, again loading our brains with more random information. The result is that we have become a culture of distracted, unfocused, overwhelmed, and stressed-out people. We're too busy.

If you are trying to reach these too-busy people, good luck. I know you want to authentically connect in a way that causes them to buy your service, subscribe to your program, donate to your cause. You may have a brilliant message, a powerful, benefit-driven offer. But it's getting lost amidst all the distraction and "mental clutter" that people are dealing with. Here's one thing you can do—SIMPLIFY!

Recently I was talking with a friend about why a particular church in town is growing so fast. What are they doing that other area churches are not? As I thought about it, I made this observation. They have made their message extremely simple—to reach people where they are and connect them to all that God has for their lives. Reach and Connect. During the announcement portion of a service, other churches may review the fifteen things that are going on that week or coming up in the month ahead. This church consistently shares just one thing— get plugged into one of their after-service action steps. That's it. Not ten things, not five or even three. One thing. They understand that for a message to get heard, remembered, and to break through the clutter of our overworked and overwhelmed brains, the message has to resonate and it has to be simple.

So this week, I encourage you to step back and consider the ways you can simplify your message. Get down to the one thing you want your customers or prospects to do ... and share that consistently well in the most simple and memorable way possible.

Too Many "Experts," Not Enough Leaders

W hen I first got married, my wife Amy and I had to work through some adjustments. She grew up in a home that was more quiet, more reserved than mine. My family is loud. We have opinions about everything and are probably too quick to share them!

These days you don't have to look too far to find someone willing to express their opinions about rioting and racial tensions, or the coronavirus, politics, or just about anything else. Social media and the multiplicity of ways we can garner information have made us all "experts" on just about any subject.

But there's a difference between being an expert and being a leader. Experts know stuff. Experts can tell you all about a situation, an event, or a topic. Leaders on the other hand know how to get you somewhere.

What does it take to be an "expert"? That's easy. Just have a good command of the information pertinent to your subject or topic and voila! You're an expert. But it takes a greater skillset to lead. Here are four traits of a leader....

1. Vision—If leadership helps people or a project get from where you are now to where you need to be, that requires vision. Leaders SEE where they need to go. They can ENVISION THE FUTURE. They can help create that vision for those that follow.

2. Perspective—Leaders know how to LISTEN, to hear the concerns, the challenges, the fears that surround a situation. The know how to EMPATHIZE, to see things from the viewpoint of others. This ability to listen, to empathize, to step outside their own mental boxes to consider other ways of doing things, other points of view, is a critical aspect of leadership.

3. Communicate—Leaders know how to INSPIRE OTHERS; they know how to cast vision, and create hope, possibility, even hunger in the minds and hearts of others by the way they communicate. Leaders have mastered the art of taking complex situations and simplifying them. Leaders are good wordsmiths.

4. Doers—Last but not least, leaders have INITIATIVE. They don't wait to be told what to do next. They figure it out and they act. Leaders don't just pontificate or get stuck in endless "analysis paralysis." In the end, leaders are WILLING TO RISK by being willing to take action.

Where's Your Focus?

Think for a minute about the people you interact with every day. Some of them are easy, reasonable, and agreeable. Then again, some of them are just plain difficult, with strong personalities or demanding agendas or odd quirks. Work, family gatherings, social situations all force us to see and interact with difficult people, sometimes people who have hurt us deeply and people who see the world very differently from how we do.

None of us is exempt from having to face difficult people. Let's be honest, we are all both flawed and fabulous at the same time. The question is, where do you choose to put your focus? If a client is grilling me about a minor problem with their book—making a proverbial mountain out of a molehill, do I choose to get resentful, critical, point out all the ways the client failed to follow our process? Or do I choose to hear what he has to say, learn from it, and as a result be a better leader, run a tighter ship, and turn out a more excellent product. You see, it really is a matter of choosing—choosing on what you focus. Do you focus on the poor delivery as your client is getting up in your grill about something insignificant? Or do you choose to listen, really hear their concerns, and make the necessary adjustments that will make you better?

Why is it some people always seem to find the good, the silver lining in a bad situation, while others almost always slip over to the dark side. I can't say I have the answer and even if I did, it would take more time than this brief letter to unpack it. Let me just encourage you to resolve to make the choice to see the glass half-full, to be a more positive and uplifting person. After all, it really is your choice. Choose to focus on the thing you can change (which is you and not the other person). And make the effort to find the fabulous in the other person. Lord knows, the flaws are there. But focusing on the flaws won't help you in your relationships. So make the choice to set your focus on the things that will brighten, lift, encourage, and help others, help the situation, and help you! You'll be glad you did.

Let's Change the Atmosphere

Every year the nation celebrates the life and achievements of Dr. Martin Luther King Jr. Dr. King was a noted civil rights leader who worked hard, even gave his life to bring equality to black people in America.

But more than serving as a civil rights icon, Dr. King fought for justice.

Let's be honest, we live in an unjust world. Life in general is not fair. You don't have to live very long or look very far before you run into injustice in some form or another. But you and I are called to "live justly, to love mercy, and walk humbly." So my challenge to both of us as we live in this unjust world is to look up, look around, and see where we can make a positive difference. Where can we change the atmosphere of our workplace, our neighborhood, our family, our community connections, by living justly and being willing to take a stand for justice.

Choosing to be just, to be fair, is not always easy. Sometimes justice comes at a cost ... to be just may require that you give up an unfair advantage that would work to your benefit. To stand up for justice may require you to step out of your comfort zone. For example, an introvert who doesn't like being in the spotlight might be called to speak up about something that's not being handled in a just and fair way. Maybe standing up for what is right costs you a friendship or a promotion. Just remember that it's not your comfort that defines you but your character. Sometimes choosing to do what's hard, what's uncomfortable, but what is right and just is the defining moment that can set you apart and change the course of your destiny, but in a good way.

So this week, this year, choose justice. Change the atmosphere around you for the better.

You Can't Manage What You Can't Measure

Earlier in my career I spent many years working for a major media company founded by a gifted entre-preneur named Stephen Strang. In my time working with Steve I learned many things, but one phrase of his that impressed me was this: "You can't manage what you can't measure." I don't know whether Steve invented that phrase or if he picked it up from someone else. All I know is that the phrase stuck with me.

In life, we all want to get better. We want to think better, do better, BE better. But how do you do that? One of the simple things you can do is to set goals for yourself. But all too often the goals we set for ourselves are nebulous, vague, and ultimately not measurable. We say things like, "I want to be the best person I can be," or "I want to lose a lot of weight," or "I want to improve my sales." Great—but if you can't state your goals in quantifiable, measurable ways, how will you know if you achieved them?

Listen, nobody particularly likes to be held accountable. But the people who get ahead in life are the ones who are willing to do just that. They push themselves. And in pushing themselves, they break their goals into measurable objectives. Why? Because you can't manage what you can't measure—and what you monitor and measure naturally tends to improve. Even if you fail to meet your stated goal, you will likely move in the right direction. So make your goals measurable: "I want to lose five pounds in the next thirty days, by limiting my calorie intake to 3,000 per day six days a week and exercising for thirty minutes at least four times a week." "I want to commit to saying at least ten positive things to at least three people every day for seven weeks until it becomes a habit." "I'm going to make at least forty outbound calls a day at least four days of the work week and send out ten new proposals a week for the next thirty days." See? Each of these statements is measurable. They are clear and specific enough for you to know whether or not you achieve them. That's accountability and it's a vital practice to master.

So pay attention to the statements, goals, and objectives that you make. Are they achievable? Are they measurable? Are they worth doing? (Yes, we sometimes set goals for ourselves that are not particularly beneficial but they make us feel good about achieving something. That's OK.) It's really up to you how hard and how often you push yourself. But when you do, make sure that your goals are measurable so you can celebrate when you achieve them!

Three Keys to Being Heard

L ast week I attended a media and broadcast convention. The exhibitors and attendees of the event
were all involved in some aspect of media—radio
programmers, television programmers, publishers,
podcasters, cable, and online streaming networks—
everyone looking to capture a wide listening, viewing,
reading audience.

Authors and leaders of various organizations were lining
up in various make-shift studios set up throughout the
convention floor for interviews by a show host, in hopes
of getting their message out to the world.

If you listened to the pitches, you would easily assume
that each of these media outlets was reaching millions of
people. And potentially they are. But the truth is, of all
the people who *could* be watching, listening, downloading
and streaming these messages, only a very small percentage of people actually are.

Just because you are speaking to a large audience doesn't mean that you are actually being heard by that audience. These days it has never been easier to get your message out to the masses. And yet, despite all the cost-effective ways to connect with others, only a small percentage of those messages are actually received by the intended audience.

So what does this mean to you? **Here are three keys to being heard.**

For starters, you have to be very selective in what you have to say. Attention spans have never been shorter. The media "noise" and level of distractions has never been higher. The art of communicating with as few words as possible is truly that ... an artform. But mastering the ability to communicate clearly and succinctly, in a way least likely to be misunderstood, in this day and age is invaluable.

Anyone who knows me well, knows I tend to ramble—I often think as I am speaking rather than before. It's not a positive trait. So this message is for me probably more than you. To break through the clutter and be heard, you have to be very succinct.

Next, you have to deliver value and results. In short, before you go into the details of all the great qualities your product or service has to offer, you need to grab attention by telling your audience first how what you have to offer will help them.

When I speak with a potential author and I ask them to tell me about their message, in most every case, they immediately jump into an enthusiastic summary of what their book is about. Stop! Nobody cares. Even when people ask you what your book, your product, or your service is about, that's not really what they are asking. What they really want to know first is whether or not what you have to offer will benefit them or help them in some way. So before you tell people what you do, be sure you first tell them how what you do will help them.

You see, we are all basically selfish creatures. We want to know more than anything if what you have to offer will benefit us in some way. Once I think that's a possibility, then I become curious to know more—then I want to know more about what it is that you do or offer. Often it is more compelling and convincing if you let others tell about the value you have to offer. Here is where testimonials and endorsements are huge. If you are the one offering the product or service, people expect you to be positive about the value it offers. But we are cynical creatures, so to alleviate that built-in suspicion, let others tell their story of how what you have to offer made a difference in their lives.

Lastly, in any communication of substance, I think it's important to be clear on what you want the recipients of your message to do. In marketing terms, you need a clear call-to-action. I see it so often in author media interviews—the author gets so excited in talking about their book, they forget to tell the audience to go out and buy a copy! Every communication you have of course does not need to end with you making a pitch to buy something—if that happens, you will quickly find people listening to you less and less.

However, when you have something important to share, when you offer someone an insight, a message, a service of unique value, then don't be shy in asking your audience to respond. I'm not saying you should be obnoxious or pushy. Just be clear in presenting what is the next best step your viewer, reader, listener can take and invite them to do so.

And now, I invite you to have an awesome rest of the week!

Are You Going the Extra Mile and Adding Value?

I recently read an e-newsletter from a friend of mine, Jim Mathis, that was so good I asked permission to share a summary with you. Here it is....

Jim was attending a conference in Portland and flew across the continent to get there. In flight, he started feeling sick—we're talking spending much of the flight in the cramped quarters of the airplane restroom. Not fun.

When Jim arrived at his destination, he limped into the downtown hotel, struggled into the lobby and practically fell across the registration desk. "Checking in?" Frank, the man at the registration desk asked with a grin ... he could tell how bad Jim felt. "Yes, but not for long. I think I've caught some 'bug' on the trip here and I am probably leaving on the first flight home tomorrow." "I'm so sorry," Frank said. "I will do everything I can to make your short stay as comfortable as possible." He quickly checked Jim in and summoned a bellman to assist with carrying luggage to the room. Once in the room Jim fell onto the bed and lay there for about twenty minutes, still aching all over. Suddenly a knock at the door, and Jim found himself facing a smiling young woman in a hotel uniform carrying a tray. "My name is Erin. Frank said you aren't feeling well, so we made you a bowl of vegetable beef soup and I included some crackers, a Sprite, and a mint. There is also a card that we all signed to help you feel better." Impressive, huh?

You see, people who add value to others become great success stories whose reputations and heritages are remembered for years. Anyone can sell, but it takes a person who adds value to people to keep their trust. Business leaders trust people who can bring resources and advice and added value to the table. Great sales are the result of becoming a business growth expert to the customer. My friend Jim was speechless! "Now you eat all of that soup, Mr. Mathis, or you won't feel better!" she scolded, like a loving mother would. After a few minutes, Jim got up, sat down, and ate the soup. Then he felt like taking a long, hot shower. Once out, he was feeling better. (Dang, Erin was right!)

Frank made an impression on Jim (as did Erin, the bellman, and the flight attendant). He tells this story as often as he can. Why? Because when people go the extra mile to add value to your life, it sticks with you.

Frank's job was to register guests with a smile, and make sure their room was available. That's all. Not order up free soup, send it up to a room, or have everyone on the staff sign a get-well card. I wish we all could be like Frank.... Jim was so moved that he called the hotel chain's customer service line when he got home and complimented Frank to the representative. She was very impressed and assured Jim that she would pass his compliment to his manager and the hierarchy.

When someone adds value to your life, you should go out of your way to express gratitude. They usually aren't looking for a compliment, but it might hit with the right person and who knows the benefit, right?

Several years ago there was a college student who studied hard to prepare for a final exam.... When the exam was passed out, he noticed it consisted only of a single sheet of paper which was blank on both sides. After the exam was passed out the professor got up and said, "I've taught you everything I can about business in the last ten weeks, but the most important message, the most important question, is this: What's the name of the lady who cleans this building?" The class didn't know the answer, and all failed the exam.

Walt Bettinger, CEO of Charles Schwab, was the student. He was a senior with a perfect 4.0 grade point average prior to that fateful test. Remembering the day, Bettinger says, "Her name was Dottie. I'd seen her, but I'd never taken the time to ask her name." Walt could have been bitter losing his perfect academic record in such a fashion, and I am sure he was disappointed. Instead, he chose to learn from the experience, stating, "It was the only test I ever failed, and I got the 'B' I deserved.... I've tried to know every Dottie I've worked with ever since." Everyone is important and worthy of respect and value.

Any time you can do more to add value to other people, your own life will be enhanced. People will flock to salespeople who go out of their way to help and become a resource for other benefits than just the sales product. Customers remember when a person goes out of their way to assist them and remember details about them to add value to the relationship.

Oh, about Frank. Ten months after Jim's hotel experience in Portland, he came back to the city to keynote for a company. He had a break one day, so he walked several blocks down the street to the hotel he had stayed in months earlier. He walked into the lobby and a woman greeted him and asked the cheerful, "Checking in?" "No, I'm looking for Frank." She obviously didn't get that question often and said, "Frank who?" "Frank, the registration guy who works here." "There's no one here by that name," she answered. Suddenly it was like a light went on in her head. "Oh, you mean FRANK! He doesn't work here any longer. He got promoted to hotel manager at another one of our hotels." And now as the famous radio host, Paul Harvey, used to say, "And now you know... the rest of the story." People like being treated special. Leaders who add value to people become great success stories whose reputations and heritages are remembered for years. Add value to your team, your customers, your clients, and watch the results roll in.

Describing the "Indescribable"

This past week my wife and I attended a "Piano Guys" concert. If you've never heard of the Piano Guys, you can check them out on YouTube. That social media platform helped launch their careers. There are four guys in the group but only two that you see on stage: a piano player, Jon Schmidt, and a cellist, Steven Sharp Nelson. These two guys are self-described middle-aged "dorky dads" but they put on an incredible show of music, conversation, and video that is well, indescribable. What they do does not fit neatly into any of the typical entertainment genres that you would expect: They are not just pop, or rock, or classical, or comedy, yet they combine all these elements into their show.

This got me thinking.... What are the unique skills, talents, insights, information that you offer?

Each of us is blessed with experiences, abilities, connections, ways of looking at things that are unique. But all too often we don't take the time to artfully find ways to express what is unique about us in ways that allow us to stand out from the competition or, on a personal level, just from other people.

Where perhaps are you selling yourself short or just not taking the time to artfully share your uniqueness in a way that will help others remember you? I have a friend, Marshall, that I meet with for breakfast on Saturday mornings at our local diner, The Townhouse. I think Marshall has some of the most insightful views on whatever issue of the day we wind up discussing. I truly think he's one of the wisest people that I know. Does he think that about himself? Nope. Does he probably miss out on opportunities to bring value and benefit to others if he would more freely share his insights? Yep. At the same time, Marshall thinks I am one of the most creative people he's ever met. Am I quick to dismiss his comments? I confess, yes.

My point is that you have unique things about you that I would challenge you to consider, not so much to boost your ego, but to enable you to be more intentional in using your unique abilities, insights, and experiences to benefit others.

What are the parts of you that are "indescribable?" Why not take some time this week to think about the indescribable things about you or your business and invest time not just identifying them but putting them into words. There is an art to taking complex people, solutions to problems, and services you offer and learning to present them in simple yet compelling ways that people can connect with and relate to. Think of the book titles *Chicken Soup for the Soul*, or *Men Are From Mars, Women Are From Venus*. Those are two great examples of finding a memorable, identifiable way of describing something that would otherwise be a rather common message—and the result is that those two books have sold millions of copies each.

I don't know about you, but I am going to invest time this week, working on ways to describe what we do at HigherLife, ways that will help people be more aware of, relate to, and potentially engage with the services we offer and the value we deliver. Will you join me?

IF YOU'RE A FAN OF THIS BOOK, WILL YOU HELP ME SPREAD THE WORD?

There are several ways you can help me get the word out about the message of this book...

• Post a 5-star review on Amazon.

• Write about the book on your Facebook, Twitter, Instagram, LinkedIn—any social media you regularly use!

• If you blog, consider referencing the book, or publishing an excerpt from the book with a link back to my website. You have my permission to do this as long as you provide proper credit and backlinks.

•Recommend the book to friends. Wword-of-mouth is still the most effective form of advertising.

• Purchase additional copies to give away as gifts.

The best way to connect with me is by: email or phone: 407-563-4806 (office) or email me at dwelday@ahigherlife.com

This book is available in deluxe hardback, paperback, eBook, and Audiobook.

 BARNES&NOBLE

ENJOY THESE OTHER
BOOKS BY DAVID WELDAY

SHAPING YOUR FAMILY STORY » At last, here is practical, non-judgmental, inspirational help for today's overworked and overwhelmed moms and dads. This book will provide you with a wealth of powerful, proven insights to help you raise great kids, whether they are 2, 12, or 20!

THE CHILDREN'S MINISTRY WORKERS' GUIDE TO EFFECTIVELY TRAINING CHILDREN » As a volunteer kids ministry worker, you don't have time to read and research how to powerfully convey spiritual truth to kids. Here is a helpful, easy-to-read guide to increasing your impact and joy in working with kids in a church setting.

HOW TO MARKET YOUR BOOK » Whether you self-publish or are working with a publisher, as the author, it's what you do to market your book that will determine its success. This helpful, practical book provides a wealth of author-directed marketing ideas and direction you can do on your own without having to spend money hiring outside help.

GET YOUR BOOK PUBLISHED! » Don't find yourself among the millions of disappointed and disillusioned authors who spend more money than they anticipated and got poorer results. This book will arm you with the vital information you need to get published while avoiding the many minefields that sideline so many great authors and messages.

CPSIA information can be obtained
at www.ICGtesting.com
Printed in the USA
LVHW081351211222
735359LV00003B/8

9 781954 533929